Howard A Kelly

RUSTY HINGES

THE AUTHOR IN TIBETAN DRESS

[*Frontispiece*

RUSTY HINGES

A STORY OF CLOSED DOORS BEGINNING TO OPEN IN NORTH-EAST TIBET

BY

FRANK DOGGETT LEARNER

F.R.G.S.

(For Twenty-two Years a Missionary in China)

THE CHINA INLAND MISSION

LONDON,   PHILADELPHIA,   TORONTO
MELBOURNE AND SHANGHAI

Agents: THE RELIGIOUS TRACT SOCIETY, 4, BOUVERIE STREET
LONDON, E.C.4
1934

First edition . . . November, 1933
Reprinted . . . . September, 1934

266
2

443

45475

MADE AND PRINTED IN GREAT BRITAIN BY PURNELL AND SONS
PAULTON (SOMERSET) AND LONDON

12646

DEDICATED
IN LIFE-LONG LOVE AND GRATITUDE
TO
MY PARENTS

BY WAY OF INTRODUCTION

IT has been my desire in recent times, strengthened by the request of many friends, to record some of the knowledge acquired and experiences passed through during the twenty years' service for His Kingdom which God has permitted me to render on the borders of Tibet.

Feeling very much my inadequacy, I venture on the task relying wholly upon God for guidance and ability, my one aim being to help create a keener missionary interest in the mysterious land of Tibet.

At the time of writing, I am sitting outside our tent on an August day at a little place among the Tibetan hills called Shang-hsin-chuang, where my wife and I have come for a few days' rest and retreat. A panorama of beautiful country is stretched out before me, the old border wall dividing Tibet from China but a few hundred yards away.

As my eyes rest on the snow-capped mountain range, from 13,000 to 15,000 feet high, I cannot but think of the millions of Tibetans on the other side who have never heard of Jesus Christ. Can I enter to the smallest degree into our Lord's yearnings as He stood on the mountain side overlooking the Holy City, "O Jerusalem, Jerusalem . . . how often would I have gathered thy children together, even as a hen gathereth her chickens under her wings, and ye would not"?

Yet one cannot say "would not" with those Tibetans beyond the glistening mountain peaks, for they have not yet had the chance of refusing.

It is they who are my plea in the task which I am facing. My experiences of the past, my work of the present, and my hopes for the future are to be my theme, and if in the end a book materializes, it will travel on its way with my eager prayer that God will show each one who reads how he or she can share in bringing our glorious Gospel to the dark, degraded, devil-worshipping people of Tibet.

FRANK DOGGETT LEARNER.

CONTENTS

ILLUSTRATIONS

xi

RUSTY HINGES

CHAPTER I

AWAY in the far north-west of China is situated the province of Tsinghai. This province was formed in the year 1928 when a large portion of western Kansu was linked to the northern section of Tibet, receiving the name of Tsinghai or Blue Lake. In this province, at an altitude of nearly 8,000 feet, and in the same latitude as the town of Seville in Spain, exquisitely situated at the juncture of four broad valleys, nestles the provincial capital, Sining,[1] "the Western City of Peace." The name seems peculiarly fitting, for during the past few years while other parts of China have been in a state of turmoil and chaos, of treachery and bloodshed, Sining has enjoyed peace and order.

Prior to this calm, however, in 1895 and 1896, Sining suffered the horrors of fire, massacre and pillage, thousands of people, Mohammedans and Chinese alike, losing their lives in the great Moslem rebellion. Since then there have been minor disturbances, which but for the wisdom and discretion of Chinese

[1] Pronounced "She-ning."

13

officials might have proved serious. In this connection it may be mentioned that Sining is an important military station, there being between twenty and thirty separate barracks in and around the city in which thousands of soldiers are quartered.

As a centre for missionary work, a better city than Sining could hardly be selected, for it possesses a commercial emporium of no mean importance, its famous market being known far and wide.

Sining also presents a unique opportunity for pioneer Gospel work among the Tibetans, for not only is it a border city but it is literally surrounded by these people. To the north, east and south, interspersed with Chinese cities, are wide districts and nomadic lands populated with Tibetans. Scattered here and there in these districts, many Tibetan lamaseries are to be found, amongst which special mention must be made of the famous lamasery of Kumbum.[1] To the west lies the great land of Tibet itself.

It will thus be seen that from a topographical standpoint Sining is uniquely situated. It may surely be called "the door of Tibet," for an important caravan route starts near the city and leads to the sacred city of Lhassa, the capital of Tibet.

In common with all Chinese cities, Sining is strongly walled. These fortifications were erected some hundreds of years ago during the Tang Dynasty. The walls are built of solid earth within, of grey burnt brick without, while the top is formed in battlement style and is wide enough to allow two or three carts

[1] Pronounced "Koomboom."

to travel abreast. The greater length of the walls is straight, but on two sides, the south and west, graceful curves present themselves. A local tradition seeking to explain this is both amusing and interesting.

One night (so the story runs) while the foundations were being laid, a fall of snow occurred. That same night a dragon passed over the newly laid foundations, trailing its course in the soft snow. It was then resolved to leave the design as the dragon's passing had formed it. Hence these curves to-day!

Let us now observe the view from the top of these historic walls. Looking outward we notice the four broad valleys already mentioned, winding their courses to north, south, east and west. They are wooded with a great variety of trees, and we see undulating fields and rounded hills, while the horizon beyond is a grandeur of snow-capped mountains glistening in the sunshine.

In great contrast is the view as one looks within the walls. It reveals one solid mass of mud-roofed houses studded here and there with both Chinese and Tibetan temples, their brightly coloured decorations and wall-painted dragons combining to give a very picturesque effect. Streets may also be seen, the two main ones intersecting in the centre of the city.

As for the population of Sining, it would be very difficult to give a correct estimate. It is many years since a census was taken, and even then it was quite unreliable. At the present day, however, it is roughly calculated that the population of Sining city and its suburbs is about 150,000.

Sining is a very cosmopolitan city. There are five distinct peoples living in the district. These are Chinese, Aboriginals, Mohammedans, Mongols and Tibetans. It goes without saying that the majority are Chinese, though there are many evidences that they were not originally in possession. Opinions vary as to which people inhabited Sining in earlier history, but there is no doubt in my own mind that Tibetans were in sole occupation. If I were asked reasons for this theory, I would point to the evacuated hermit caves, to decaying Tibetan relics, and especially to the remains of the old border wall some miles west of the city. It is of added interest that this wall in its crumbling condition, although many centuries old, is traceable throughout its entire length.

As this little volume is to be devoted almost exclusively to Tibet and the Tibetans, but limited space can be given to the other four races of people. A few facts, however, may be recorded.

1. *THE CHINESE* of Sining originally came from the province of Anhwei, but having lived in Kansu for many centuries, they now differ much in speech and appearance from the people of that province. They are very lovable and extremely kind and hospitable. On the whole they are poor but at the same time independent. Nor are they so cunning and crafty as the Chinese of other parts are reputed to be. Owing in some degree to illiteracy, they are often indifferent to the Gospel, but once they have been persuaded they become sterling Christians.

[Photo by F. Doggett Learner

THE OLD BORDER WALL BETWEEN CHINA AND TIBET

[Facing page 16

SHANG-HSIN-CHUANG

[Photo by F. Doggett Learner

The place among the hills on the border of China and Tibet where *Rusty Hinges* began to be written.

2. *THE MOHAMMEDAN* population of the former Kansu province numbers approximately three millions. Generally speaking they are distinguished by their tall stature, their broad features, their closely cut moustaches and bushy beards, their brisk movements, and their hexagonal black or white caps. Through intermarriage with the Chinese, they have lost their racial characteristics to a certain extent, though they preserve evident traces of their western origin, having come from Arabia, Turkey and Persia, as well as from Mongolia.

(*a*) Firstly, there are Mohammedans of *Arabian* origin, and these outnumber the other groups by many thousands. They came to the district during the Tang Dynasty.[1] For the most part they congregate in and around Hochow, a beautifully situated city known as the "Mecca of China." These people are prosperous and enterprising men of business. It is sometimes said that a Mohammedan with a tray of peanuts makes more noise and bustle than a Chinese with a large store.

As a rule those who belong to this race of Mohammedans have a knowledge of Arabic, and some are so well versed in it as to be able to speak it fluently. Among this latter class are the *ahongs*, or priests, who are also able to expound the text of the Koran. Evangelistic work has been carried on for some years among these people by the China Inland Mission.[2]

[1] A.D. 618–907
[2] The Rev. and Mrs. G. K. Harris and Mr. L. A. Street have been set apart especially for this work in the Sining district.

B

(*b*) The Mohammedans of *Turkish* origin are often known as Salars. It is said that this group came to the district during the Ming Dynasty,[1] and thus at a much later date than those from Arabia. These people migrated directly from Samarkand and settled in the district three or four days' journey south-east from Sining. They are fierce and fearless. Owing to their daring they have proved themselves excellent soldiers. They speak their own language, the majority knowing no Chinese and little Arabic. Their clothes are in semi-Tibetan style though the women folk retain the dress of Samarkand. They often visit our "Gospel Hall," but we feel our helplessness in preaching to them as we do not know their language. Surely a harvest is waiting to be reaped from among them! Did not our Lord command that the Gospel be preached to "every creature"? It cannot be that these Salars should be left out.

(*c*) The *Persian* Mohammedans migrated from their own country some centuries ago. Having to a great extent forgotten their own language, they mostly speak Chinese. Many thousands of these people are to be found in the regions west of Sining.

(*d*) Then there is a wide district to the east and south-east of Hochow which is populated by a people under the general name of *Mongol* Moslems. They are of smaller stature than the Arabian and Turkish Moslems, and many of them have brown hair and eyes. They can speak Chinese fluently, though the Tartar language is much used among themselves.

[1] A.D. 1368–1644

(e) Lastly we must mention the *Chinese* Mohammedans who are found more or less all over China.
As the name indicates, these are Chinese who have
embraced the Moslem religion.

The earnestness of all Mohammedans in following
the Prophet surely puts to shame many a disciple
of Jesus Christ. It has been rightly said that every
Moslem is a missionary, for old and young, rich and
poor alike, seem never to tire in striving to further
the cause of their religion.

In Sining, the Mohammedans for the most part
live in the suburbs, and this for the simple reason
that until recent years they have not been allowed
within the city. The eastern suburb, where the
Moslem General has his residence, is almost exclusively peopled with Mohammedans of whom there
are many thousands.

The chief mosque is in this suburb, and worship
is held regularly five times daily. At dawn, at noon,
two hours before sunset, at sunset, and two hours
after sunset, the muezzin cry, "There is no god
but God, and Mohammed is the Prophet of God,"
rings out its call to prayer at this mosque as over
the whole Moslem world.

Friday is observed as the Moslem Sabbath (*Chu-ma*),
and the mosque is especially full at the noon service
when the Moslem General in command of the troops
attends in person. For his other hours of devotion, the
General's own priest officiates. This *ahong* accom-
panies him everywhere so that he may be at hand
when the call to worship sounds.

The Moslem creed is chiefly concerned with God,

His angels, His books, His prophets, His day of Judgment and Predestination. Ramazan, the month of fasting, is religiously observed by all. During this time no drop of water or morsel of food may be taken while daylight lasts. Hunger is abundantly satisfied, however, after dark.

3. *THE ABORIGINALS* of the Sining district, commonly known among the Chinese as "the people of the soil," are a primitive race and may engage our attention in passing. They inhabit the plains, valleys and mountains of a district north-east of Sining. It is believed that they migrated from Mongolia during the Tang Dynasty. The story is told that a Mongol king named Li-chin-wang led them in a campaign against the Tibetans. As a proof of this, a slab of stone marking the grave of this king may be seen on the bank of the river two days' journey to the east of Sining. The story of their migration is inscribed on the stone, and from it we learn that Li-chin-wang had thirteen sons who became the leaders of thirteen clans which are still existent. These clans are distinguished by the thirteen styles of hats worn by the women folk, the hats being similar to those worn by the thirteen wives of the thirteen princes. They are mostly orange in colour. That of the eldest son's clan is very cumbersome. It is decorated with brass ornaments and weighs about five pounds.

The language of the Aboriginals is a mixture, containing many words derived from both Tibetan and Turkish. Up to the present, it has not been reduced to writing, but we look forward to the time when this will be possible. The Aboriginals are an accessible people, and we give thanks that a few of them are already connected with our Church. How we long that some in the homeland may hear God's call to give themselves to this most important work!

4. *THE MONGOLS* in the district are comparatively few. For the most part they are visitors coming from Mongolia either for purposes of trade, or as pilgrims to Kumbum. This sacred city is a great centre of attraction, and at times of specified religious festivals we have seen thousands of Mongols bound for it. They travel by camel, and their caravans stretch for long miles along the winding valley roads leading to Kumbum. It is a very picturesque sight to watch them as they wend their way with their bedding and other paraphernalia, as well as their persons, on camel-back.

The dress of the Mongolians is not unlike that of the Tibetans, though it is easily distinguishable to the trained eye. That of the men folk generally consists of four articles, namely, a thick sheepskin gown worn next to the body, a pair of skin trousers, a fur hat and leather boots, which, with a match-lock thrown over the right shoulder, complete the picture. In stature, they are thick set and strongly knit, with brawny arms and muscular chests which are exposed to sun and wind alike. Their faces are generally pleasant, though stern.

Not a few Mongols are found as lamas in the lamaseries around Sining, but otherwise there are few residing in the district. Evangelistic work among

these people is very difficult, as we know nothing
of their language, and they do not speak Chinese.
All we can do is to attempt to place the printed
Word of God in their hands, both in Mongolian and
Kalmuk, the former for those from Mongolia, the
latter for those from the Russian border.

.   .   .   .   .

Before leaving the Western City of Peace, the early
stages of Gospel work there may briefly be told.
Sining was opened as a Mission station in the year
1885. The stories handed down by the early missionaries are deeply interesting, and through them
we can understand something of the difficulties
contended with, the fidelity of the labourers shining
through like threads of gold.

Preaching on the streets was no easy matter in
early times, for although curious crowds collected,
yet as soon as the name of Jesus was mentioned, the
company dispersed. Sometimes a bookstall was set
up with the hope of distributing the Scriptures among
the people. Passers-by came round, and often were
almost persuaded to take a copy. Now unfortunately
some Chinese have a habit of smelling an article
before buying it. Thus it happened frequently that
a would-be purchaser of a Gospel raised the booklet
to his nasal organ. As the people were illiterate,
they were unacquainted with the odour of printer's
ink, and with a grimace of disgust the book was
hastily thrown down, and there was no more chance
of other people accepting books or tracts for a while.
I myself have seen the above incident happen, even
in recent years.

Unpleasant rumours were afloat, too, that the queer-looking foreigners surreptitiously snatched babies from their homes and boiled them for making medicines; that if someone was photographed by them, his spirit was snapped or enticed into the camera; that Condy's fluid (which may be found in all mission dispensaries), was the blood of the unfortunates who had been captured by the "foreign devil." These and many other like stories show us that for the early missionaries pioneering work was very hard.

As the years slipped by and not a soul was won, would not the labourers weary of their task? But God was going to use a special way to open the door of the people's hearts—the way of a little child in the midst. He gave to Mr. and Mrs. Ridley[1] a baby girl. Now the inhabitants of Sining had never seen a pink and white western baby before. Little Dora was proudly carried through the streets of the city, and a miracle happened. Whereas formerly doors had been shut in their faces, now they were opened wide, and people ran out to see the wonderful little scrap of humanity, crowding round to look at the golden hair and blue eyes and fair pinky skin.

Invitations for visits to the homes of the people now came pouring in, and the missionaries had as many opportunities as they could use. Thus the barrier was broken down, and the way for evangelism was clear—and all through an innocent babe!

A Guest Room had been opened in the Gospel Hall long before, but no one had dared come in.

[1] Mr. and Mrs. Ridley reached Sining in July, 1894.

Now there were frequent visitors, and according to Chinese ceremony tea was served to each guest. Yet even this politeness was sometimes regarded with suspicion, for some said that the foreigners' tea was drugged so that the recipient was made a Christian against his will.

The year 1904, nearly two decades after Sining had been opened as a Mission station, will never be forgotten, for it was during that year that the first three people were received into the Church by baptism. From that time the Church continued growing— opposition gradually diminished, favour was won, and confidence gained.

In the year 1914, ten years after the first three baptisms, my wife and I were greatly honoured and privileged in being allocated to Sining, each of us having previously spent two or three years in other parts of the province. At that time the church roll stood at nearly fifty members. To-day the register contains close on three hundred names, and each of the five before-mentioned peoples are represented on that roll. Surely a striking witness of God's wonder-working power!

Many a page could be filled with the record of work among the Chinese of Sining and district, but these writings are to be devoted to Tibet and her peoples. Therefore we will now turn to our main theme—a mysterious land and race enveloped in obscurity!

CHAPTER II

STRANGE to say, the name Tibet is quite unknown to the Tibetans! To themselves, their land is known as "Wod Yul", or the Land of the Barbarians. It is said that the designation of Tibet was given by the Turks.

Roughly speaking, Tibet is about eight times the size of Great Britain, having an area of over 700,000 square miles. It has been rightly styled "The Great Closed Land", for it is surrounded by mountains. On the north are the Kuen Luen heights. On the west is the Karakorum range. Chinese mountains form a boundary on the east, while on the south are the great Himalayas. All these mountains are of great height, many of the peaks rising to 20,000 feet, while Mount Everest on the south-eastern boundary of Tibet is, as every one knows, 29,000 feet above sea level.

Tibet has been called "the largest mass of rock in the world." Its lowest altitude is well over 10,000 feet above sea level, and many of its tablelands rise to over 17,000 feet in height. To impress on our minds the most important fact in its physical geography, namely its great elevation, let us remember that the average height of Tibet is greater than that of Mont Blanc!

It is somewhat difficult for the average foreigner to live at such altitudes. By way of illustration, a rather unpleasant personal experience may be told. Some years ago, when travelling over the border, we had stayed at a certain place for some days and were congratulating ourselves that we had not been affected by the altitude. One night I lay sleepless, and feeling the air of the over-heated room oppressive, I went out for a stroll in the fresh keen air of a temple courtyard. I do not know for how long I walked around, but I suddenly awoke to find myself lying on the cold hard stones of the temple yard. I must have fallen senseless to the ground! After that, I could no longer claim to be insusceptible to the altitude.

Concerning the population of Tibet, it is impossible to give a correct estimation. One census taken in the seventeenth century gave the figure at nearly two millions, but a more modern estimate makes it five millions. This is, however, a most debatable point.[1]

Tibet is divided into three sections, namely, Great Tibet, Tibet Proper, and Little Tibet.

The part of Great Tibet which is now included in the newly-formed Tsinghai province is of no mean size. It includes the great Koko-nor Lake. Several new towns are growing up in this region which will one day become important centres.

[1] The latest estimate published by the Chinese Ministry of the Interior gives the figure 3,720,000.

Yu-shu-hsien, a city about four hundred miles from Sining by a fairly good motor road, is nearly half way to Lhassa. The route is to be connected through to the sacred city in time.

Tibet Proper is in the centre of the great land. It contains the two great provinces of U and Tsang, the latter including Lhassa where the Dalai Lama, the head of Buddhism in Tibet, has his palace and home.

Little Tibet is on the west or Indian side. It comprises five small provinces, three of which are dependencies of Kashmir, while the other two belong to Britain.

The climate of Tibet is, as may be expected, very cold, though owing to the vastness of its territory it differs with latitude and season. For five or six months of the year, arctic conditions prevail over the whole country. On the other hand, there is a very short and excessively hot summer, especially in the valleys of the Indus and Sanpo. Winters are intensely severe. The thermometer between dark and dawn continuously registers below zero, while frequently it falls 20 deg. or 30 deg. lower. One time, when travelling in Tibet in the month of January, a daily experience was to find our bread frozen so hard that a knife would make no impression. One had to hack off a small piece and then hold it in one's mouth until thawed. Another time I recall opening a tin of sardines, but only to find a block of ice which had to be melted before use. Thus the intensity of the cold is difficult to contend with while travelling. On one occasion, in addition to my usual heavy winter clothing, I wore two extra gowns, one of which was thickly lined with fur, and even then I suffered miserably with cold.

The Tibetans have a successful if novel way of warding off the cold. They smear the whole body over with butter, thus protecting themselves from the prevalent bitter winds and arctic temperature. As may be surmised, they diffuse fragrance wherever they go. We have had visitors in our living rooms in Sining who have left their odoriferousness behind them long after their departure.

Tibet can boast of giving rise to five of the world's greatest rivers. On the south the Brahmaputra, the Ganges and the Indus have their source, while the springs of the Yangtzekiang and the Yellow river may be found on the east. The land is rich with many other rivers. There are seventy-two which feed the great Koko-nor alone. This immense lake is 230 miles in circumference. Owing to its having no outlet, its deep blue waters are very salt. It is situated at an altitude of 10,000 feet. Five islands may be seen above its blue waters, the largest of which contains a lamasery. Many other lakes of no mean size are to be found in Tibet, next in importance being those of Tengri and Chargut.

Tibet has an active trade with surrounding countries, commerce being in the hands of rich Tibetan and Chinese merchants. The chief exports are sheep's wool, hides and furs, dried apricots and dates, antelope horns and yak tails, rhubarb root and incense, as well as the minerals gold, silver, zinc, mercury, sulphur and salt. A truly wonderful land for the enterprising trader!

Among the imports are tea, rice, sugar, spices, tobacco and grain, tents, leather boots, saddles and fire-arms, in addition to which may be mentioned coral and brocade for the gratification of the Tibetan aesthetic taste.

Export and import trade is carried on by means of caravan routes traversing the country. Merchandise of every sort is transported on yak, and it is a fascinating sight to watch the high road leading to Tibet with the long trails of yak laden with merchandise. This road ever presents a scene of energy and bustle, especially in the winter months when great quantities of sheep's wool are transported by countless yak from the uttermost parts of Tibet.

Agriculture is a difficult art in Tibet. The east is far too bleak and unsheltered, fearful winds sweeping across the land rendering the soil barren and unfit for cultivation. In the north are vast steppes where pasture innumerable herds of wild animals—undisturbed by man—yak, horses, asses, goats and antelopes.

In the west, however, the weather is warmer and crops may be grown with apparent success. Barley is the chief product, for from it is made the staple food of Tibet—*tsamba*. Wheat, rye, peas and beans are grown in lesser quantities.

In the south, there are extensive orchards of apricot trees. The fruit is exported in a dried form, and an oil extracted from the trees is used both for lighting and toilet purposes.

The whole of Tibet offers a wonderful field to the botanist. The mountains, as well as the plains, are full of every species of wild flower, from the tiny primula of white, pink and purple hue, to the great rhododendron which has been seen growing to enormous heights. Raspberries, strawberries and gooseberries in their wild state abound in the lower hills. These make good jam for the missionary.

Birds of all species are found in Tibet. On several occasions, we have had the pleasure of welcoming ornithologists to our Sining home, and each one has asserted that the opportunities for study and exploration are limitless.

Many fine specimens of the eagle are to be found, amongst which may be mentioned the sacred black eagle. This is a scavenger bird and is used for the disposal of the dead. The golden eagle and a white-headed specimen are more beautiful, and as they hover above in the sunshine, their feathers glisten like gold and silver.

Falcons are tamed, and then trained to catch rabbits and pheasants. Mohammedan soldiers frequently use the falcon for this purpose, carrying it on the forearm.

The peacock is a sacred bird to the Tibetans. The feathers of the tail are used in worship and are conspicuous in every lamasery. Vultures, kites and hawks, pheasants, cranes, ducks and geese, besides innumerable specimens of smaller birds, are to be found in great abundance.

Fish are numerous. In the rivers trout are to be found, and Scottish anglers would delight to cast a fly in the streams after rain. The Tibetan method of catching fish is both simple and primitive. The process is carried out in winter only, when the lakes are frozen. Holes of a foot or two in diameter are bored through the ice, and after dark the fishermen stand around the holes holding lanterns. The fish are attracted to the light, and it is then a very simple matter to scoop them out with nets. Sometimes this is not necessary, for the fish, allured by the light, themselves leap out of the hole.

According to the religious beliefs of the Tibetans, fish are considered unclean and the people do not eat them in any shape or form. A brisk trade, however, is carried on during the winter months between the Koko-nor and Sining, the buying and selling being mostly in the hands of Mohammedans and Chinese.

Fishing, if a lucrative occupation, is sometimes a dangerous one. Among the many patients coming to our city dispensary, a man with his hand bound up appeared one day. On removing the rags, a hideous laceration on the back of his hand came to view. The flesh seemed to have been torn from the bone, which was fully exposed. On being questioned, the man told us that the wound had been made by a fish. While he was landing it, the fish had bitten his hand! We could scarcely believe the story, but there was no reason why the man should concoct a fabrication.

Many species of wild beasts are to be found in Tibet. Panthers, leopards, tigers, bears and wolves, as well as the more harmless camels, foxes, wild asses and smaller animals—these all roam at will in the steppes and mountain regions.

But one cannot leave the fauna of Tibet without a paragraph about the yak. The dictionary describes the yak as a species of ox, but in appearance it rather resembles the bison. Another definition

is that of a grunting ox because it never ceases to
grunt. It is similar in height to an English short-
horn, standing at about five and a half feet. It is
massive in structure, has short legs, long thick curved
horns and bull-like neck. Its chief characteristic,
however, is its thick coat of long hair which may
be either white, grey or black, and which often
reaches the ground. It also has an enormous tail
covered with a prodigious amount of long silky
hair.

In its wild state, the yak is a fierce, untamable
beast. If attacked, it rushes upon its enemy with
lowered horns, using its chest to crush its victim.
Wild yak roam the mountain heights and plateaux
in enormous herds, and the Tibetans think it best
to leave them alone. In the less cold summer months,
finding warmth intolerable, they escape to inaccess-
ible heights in the region of perpetual snow.

The domesticated yak is of a different nature and
is an indispensable animal to the Tibetans. Most
of the nomads own large herds, which are their
chief wealth. They flourish only at an altitude of
10,000 feet or over, and if taken to a lower level,
they succumb. The following anecdote will serve
as proof of this statement. A few years ago, a wealthy
Tibetan living near Sining, wishing to add to his
store of riches, hired men to take one hundred yak
from Sining to Peking for sale. The story ends here,
for every one of the animals died on the way!
The only compensation my friend obtained was
the knowledge that it would not pay to repeat the
experiment.

The domesticated yak is of great value to the Tibetan. The coarser hair is used for the manufacture of their tents, while the finer is woven into more delicate fabrics. Yak tails have an important market. Of late years they have been exported to Japan, the hair being used for weaving purposes, while the meat is converted into tinned oxtail soup. The female animal gives very good milk, and the Tibetans use it continually in the making of their tea, as well as butter. Yak meat, though sometimes tough, is very good, and is an everyday food of the people.

But the chief value of the domesticated yak lies in its employment as a pack animal. It is very surefooted and can keep its hold where a horse or mule would find it an impossibility. Carrying a load up to 150 lbs. in weight, it can safely tread over dangerous paths and precipitous mountain passes. It is also used as a riding animal, but the back of a yak is most decidedly not the safest way to travel, for its temper is none of the best. Were it not for a wooden ring piercing its nose, with a rope attached, it would be altogether uncontrollable. Even with this rein, the beast may suddenly rush up a steep bank, regardless of whom or what it carries, and both the rider and the pack may be found in a huddled heap on the ground. Or when crossing through a river, it may suddenly desire to take a roll in the waters, and the unfortunate rider must of necessity have a cold splash too!

In bringing this chapter to a conclusion, a brief word may be said about the government of Tibet.

c

Of its early history, much has been written in the past, the records going back to the seventh century when Buddhism was introduced into Tibet from India.

Tibet was originally an independent kingdom ruled by hereditary kings. As the result of a conspiracy against the presiding king during the eighteenth century, it became indirectly subject to China, which country has claimed a suzerainty over it since that time. Thus all Tibetan affairs are under the paramount authority of the executive force at the Chinese capital.

At a later date, national government was committed to the Dalai Lama (literally "Sea of Wisdom"), the sovereign pontiff, who resides at the Potala, or palace, at Lhassa. Being considered supreme in Buddhist hierarchy, his judgment is absolute in dealing with all affairs whether political or religious.[1] In local matters, Tibetan chiefs bear the brunt of the work, though they are subject to the Dalai Lama. They are also responsible for the collecting of taxes from their districts. As Tibet has no coin currency, these taxes are levied in kind. Grain, wool, furs, hides, cattle and horses are some of the articles collected in taxation. No official salaries are paid to the chiefs, but they tax the people over and above what is due, making ample deduction for their own use before handing on to headquarters.

[1] At the present moment (September 1934) Tibet is passing through a period of political instability following upon the death of the Dalai Lama in December, 1933.

CHAPTER III

THE PEOPLE OF TIBET

THE Tibetans are a stalwart, frank and fearless people. Taken as a whole, they have many pleasing characteristics. They are good-natured, and have a happy, cheerful disposition. They are comparatively truthful though they are quick at fault-finding. When quarrelling among themselves—and they argue over trifles—they can use very scurrilous language. They live unrestrained lives, and all more or less could be charged with immorality, drunkenness, lubricity and cruelty.

In their contact with missionaries in Sining city they have proved themselves very friendly, while in my travels over the border their kindness and hospitality have warmed my heart. On the other hand, I have met with ill-will and hostility more than once.

The Tibetans are sturdily built, with well-developed chest, brawny arms and muscular legs. They have a brachycephalic skull with high forehead and cheekbones. Big brown or hazel eyes, strong white teeth and very thick lips are noticeable, while added to these may be mentioned a broad flat nose with huge nostrils, the last partly accounted for by their excessive use of snuff.

Their hair is usually seen in dishevelled plaits. A certain religious sect never cut or comb their hair, and it is left to grow at will. It is twisted into coils which are loosely wound round the head. When let down, they trail on the ground for several feet looking like dirty black ropes. They are verminous withal.

No beard or moustache is worn, though the process of shaving is unknown. All hair on the face is removed by tweezers, which are always carried on the person. If a single hair dares to appear during sleep, the morning sees it speedily removed. When in conversation with Tibetans, I have often seen them at work with the tweezers, pulling here and there almost unconsciously at refractory sprouts!

Their skin is reddish brown, this partly due to exposure, and partly perhaps to never having washed. It is difficult to say just what the natural complexion really is!

The typical dress of the nomadic people consists of five articles, namely, a long sheepskin gown or robe, a girdle, a pair of huge rough leather boots, and fur or coarse cotton trousers. A shirt is sometimes worn by the more refined. The gown would reach the ground were it not for the girdle, which is bound tightly round the waist, the robe being looped up and hanging down over the girdle, forming a gigantic pocket in which a multitude of accessories is always kept.

The nomads especially have a paraphernalia of articles always with them, some inside the pocket and some out. Among them may be mentioned a string of beads, usually in the hand, a Buddha box worn on the chest, a prayer wheel, a tinder outfit, a pewter wine-bottle, a knife, a pipe and tobacco box, a sewing outfit, a stone snuff-box, and a few *khata*, or scarves of salutation.

The pocket, however, is often used for other purposes. I have frequently seen chunks of butter, as well as other eatables, emerging from its voluminous folds. One day a Tibetan visitor was in my office in Sining. During our conversation, I noticed him fumbling around in his pocket as if in search of something. Suddenly he whipped out a raw leg of mutton, and thrust it into my arms explaining that it was a present. I thanked him with a very broad smile which I was able to keep in control until he was gone, when my wife and I had a good laugh.

A change from winter to summer attire is easily accomplished by slipping, according to the temperature, either one or both arms from the sleeves of the gown. This allows the garment to fall loosely around the body, exposing arms, shoulders and chest to the sun and winds of heaven.

The better class Tibetans dress differently from the nomads. They are usually clad in a woollen cloth called a *pulu*, which is made on a hand loom, and comes from the western part of the country. This material resembles a thick merino, and is very durable. It is generally seen in plain colours, though some of it has a cross pattern on it. The method of producing the chequered design is both simple and ingenious. Material of plain colour is folded or pleated in such a way that when it is dipped in a contrasting dye, a cross effect is imprinted on the original cloth. The dyes are fast, for neither rain nor sun seems to affect them. A good *pulu* is very expensive, and sufficient cloth for one robe may cost as much as £20. In the most severe weather, the wealthy Tibetans line their gowns with either lamb or fox skin. Sometimes the edges of the garment, and the collar and cuffs, are ornamented with strips of tiger, leopard or panther skin. The effect is very handsome.

Silks and satins may sometimes be seen instead of *pulu*, the chief colours being red or gold. The women of the wealthy usually dress in gorgeous silks, and they wear much jewellery. Ornaments of gold, silver, amber, coral, turquoise, agates and pearls are all seen in abundance, whether for rings, bracelets, necklaces or earrings. The last are especially conspicuous, and often three or four of them are suspended from each ear. Chinese silver dollar coins are also used as ornaments. Men as well as women wear rings and bracelets. I have also frequently seen a man wearing one earring in the right ear. It is generally of silver studded with coral and turquoise.

The ladies' hair attracts one's notice. It is often worn in 108 plaits, which number represents that of their main sacred books. From the hair may be suspended several pounds' weight of silver ornaments. Heavy shells are worn in the same way. One wonders whether these women ever suffer from headache!

A WEALTHY
TIBETAN LADY

The back view shows
ornaments suspended
from the hair.

[Photo by J. T. Mathewson

A TYPICAL TIBETAN NOMAD

Finger-nail protectors on the third and little fingers of both hands are also worn by men and women of high rank. The nails are allowed to grow several inches long, to indicate that no manual labour wears them down.

Hats of every possible or impossible shape are devised, whether of fur, silk, cloth or straw. Some have peaks, some tassels, some earflaps. In winter, the favourite material is fur. Often I have seen the whole skin of a fox wound round the head, but it is usually fashioned into a wearable shape, and when lined with silk makes a very comfortable cap. If no hat is available, a piece of sheepskin or an old cloth is wrapped round the head, the latter doing duty for a handkerchief as well.

The priests' dress differs from that of the people, the yellow and red sects being easily distinguished by the colour of their clothing. A long shawl wrap several yards in length wound loosely round the shoulders, a waistcoat, a skirt, and boots made of cloth or leather are the four articles which complete the outfit. During prayer times, a long cloak and tall yellow hat, the top of which resembles a cock's comb, are added. The dress of Incarnate Buddhas, though more elaborate, is much like that of the priests, except that exquisite embroidery decorates it.

There is not much variety in the food of the Tibetans. Mutton and yak beef are eaten daily. Pork, fish and chicken are forbidden by their religion. Priests are not allowed to eat flesh in any shape or form, but this does not mean that they refrain from it, for I have frequently seen priests at the meat stalls in the market places. More mutton is eaten than beef, for the reason that yak are used as beasts of burden, as well as for milking purposes. They are only killed when diseased or past work.

Some years ago, I was passing through a certain place and saw a cow being skinned. I asked for what reason it had been killed. I shall never forget the disdainful look on the man's face!

"Why, it died of itself!" he replied.

"And what are you going to do with it?" I asked.

"Eat it, of course! What else should we do with it?" came the scornful rejoinder. I wondered whether he thought I was mentally affected.

When a diseased beast is killed, prayers are chanted by the priest. The whole of the animal is used. There is no waste. Its skin is converted into leather. Every possible part of the animal is eaten. The entrails, after cleansing, are filled with a mixture of heart, liver, and kidney combined with barley flour and vegetable oil. I have found this a palatable and very appetizing dish when served hot. Scotsmen might be reminded of haggis. In the case of mutton, the tail is considered the tastiest piece, and is always put before the visitor as a special mark of respect. If from a big sheep, it weighs about two pounds and is practically all fat.

Wheat is eaten very little in eastern Tibet, as the climate is too severe to grow it. All that is consumed is brought over the border, and is therefore expensive.

The Chinese in Sining city sell wheaten flour to
Tibetans, but there is a great amount of cheating
in the transaction. I have watched the process.
The flour is kept in a semi-dark room at the back
of the shop, and the Tibetan, carrying his leathern
sack, is taken there. True, he witnesses the meal
being measured and emptied into his sack, but
with cunning dexterity, the passing through many
hands, and the accompaniment of much shouting
and bustle, little more than half the flour bought
finds its way into the Tibetan's sack. Surely "the
quickness of the hand deceives the eye!" The
Tibetan, handicapped by his imperfect knowledge
of the Chinese language, and as a stranger in a strange
land, dares not object.

Barley flour made into *tsamba* is one of the
chief foods in Tibet. The grain is first baked, and
then ground into flour. A quantity of meal is put
(as required) into a bowl in which tea and butter
have been placed. When mixed with the fingers
into the consistency of dough, it is taken out and
eaten as it is. This is *tsamba*. We missionaries
fortunately get to like it quite well. In a thinner
consistency it makes a good substitute for porridge.

Tibetans are great tea drinkers. The tea is carried
up by cart or mule back from Hankow, a distance
of many hundred miles. Hankow is famous for its
tea, but the finer qualities are either exported to
foreign countries or are used in north and west
China. What reaches Tibet is in "brick" form,
that is, tea leaves pounded into oblong cakes, each
weighing about eight pounds. It is of very inferior

quality, and evidently contains the sweepings of the warehouses, for one always sees a sediment of mud at the bottom of one's tea bowl.

Were the reader to be suddenly offered a cup of Tibetan tea, I fear he would not recognize it as such. He would most probably think it was soup, which it doubtless resembles, for milk, salt and butter are added freely, and it is often boiled several hours before it is served.

For a special guest, butter preserved for several years is produced, and extra pats are dropped into his tea bowl by mine host himself. The visitor who wishes to show his appreciation of the honour bestowed upon him, bows and smiles, and passes his bowl many times for refilling. When all are satisfied, each one licks his cup completely clean in readiness for the next occasion.

At meal times the whole family, young and old alike, gather round the pot. Spoons and forks are unknown to the Tibetan, and chopsticks are seldom seen. By means of the fingers, each one helps himself to the chunks of meat from the boiling cauldron. Tibetans have enormous appetites, and they seem to have no difficulty in disposing of several pounds of meat at a sitting. The foreign visitor gets a lean time, as he cannot dip his fingers easily into the seething broth of the cauldron, though he is glad of an excuse to eat less than his hosts. When so far satisfied, each one produces his bowl from the gigantic pocket, and proceeds to ladle out the soup. Many bowls of the savoury mixture are drunk, after which they are well licked and returned clean to the pocket.

Greasy fingers are wiped on the hair, and the meal is complete.

Cleanliness is foreign to Tibetans, for they abhor water, and from the day of birth to that of death they are never washed. Butter only is used for toilet purposes, the whole of the body being smeared with it from time to time, while the face, hands and chest are lubricated daily. The end justified by the means, for dust clings to the butter, and an outer crust is formed, protecting the skin from the bitter penetrating winds. One might think that this form of toilet might be altered in warmer weather, but such is not the case. I have seen a Tibetan on a hot summer day with glistening countenance, melted butter trickling down face and chest, and dribbling from his hands. Fortunately for the missionary, the Tibetan form of salutation is not that of handshaking!

Tibetan butter, alas, is far from clean, for it often has dirty yak hairs embedded in it. It is formed with the hands, and not by churn. When made, it is pressed into skins and bladders for preservation. This enables it to be kept for longer or shorter periods. As the years pass, the butter becomes greener and greener, reminding one of gorgonzola cheese of greater or lesser maturity. It is made in pieces of varying size. Once in a certain Tibetan encampment I wanted a small pat of freshly made butter, but all that was procurable was an ancient lump of about fifty pounds weight.

Tibetans are inordinately fond of wine, tobacco and snuff. The wine is usually from barley distillation, and comes from over the China border. Drunkenness, with all its corrupting influence, is sadly common. The tobacco is fortunately mild and harmless. The pipes are long, and they usually have amber mouth-pieces, and very tiny cups of bronze or brass. Another kind, made of metal, is known as the "water-pipe," as the smoke passes through water before entering the mouth. This is considered a very clean way of smoking, and the water is changed daily. Snuff is used to excess. When friend meets friend, snuff boxes are invariably produced. If this exchange of greetings is lacking, some trouble is certainly brewing! It is ever a wonder to our Tibetan friends that their western guests do not enjoy a sniff!

Opium smoking is unknown to Tibetans.

Tibetan salutations are both interesting and unique. Two friends meet, and simultaneously their two tongues shoot out, hanging down on their chins. At the same instant, two pairs of thumbs are held up perpendicularly. Then, the bodies bent slightly forward, each says to the other, "Aro, demo ing?", (Friend, how are you?), and finally, all four hands extended, the scarves of salutation, or *khata*, are exchanged.

Friendly intercourse follows, and were the reader a bystander, he would be both amused and interested at the many gesticulations, denoting pleasure or otherwise. In expressing delight, the right ear is pulled, while the left hand vigorously rubs the hip. The tongue frequently darting out is likewise a sign of pleasure, but if a little finger is held up, offence is indicated. A Tibetan's tongue seems to be of abnormal length, probably due to the fact that its muscles are so frequently in use. He can bring it down to the full length of his chin, and he doubtless thinks that of the westerner is very insignificant.

The *khata* are white or sky blue in colour, and are made either of cotton or silk, with ravelled ends. They vary much in quality and texture, as well as in length. A small cotton scarf costs but a few cents, while a larger one of silken gauzy material may be worth several dollars. Figures of Buddha are woven into the most costly *khata*.

Besides being used in salutation, no present is ever given unless a *khata* is spread over it. Its absence would be a breach of refinement. When travelling in Tibet, it is wise to be well supplied with scarves. Fortunately, it is not an expensive item, as for every *khata* given another is received in exchange.

Presentation of *khata* to idols in temples is a common occurrence. Once I remember seeing a brightly coloured idol draped with soft blue and white silken scarves, and a very pleasing effect was produced.

The chief occupation of the Tibetans is that of attending their flocks and herds. They are rich in cattle, and some of the wealthy nomads own literally thousands of head of cattle. The animals are mostly yak and sheep, although numbers of horses are owned too.

Amusements for Tibetans are few. Throwing dice and playing with cards indicates their passion for gambling, and I have even known the long sheepskin gown to be a wager. Singing and dancing are favourite pastimes too, and are often made very hilarious by the presence of the wine bottle. Tibetan singing is quite fascinating when heard from a distance. As one travels along any of the beaten tracks, Tibetan girls may be heard singing on the mountains as they watch their flocks. Their voices seem to carry for miles across the plains.

One custom in singing seems to me peculiar to Tibet. Two young women sit facing each other so closely as to enable their noses to touch. As they sing together in unison, their voices are echoed and re-echoed from each other's throats. The effect of the two voices blending as if in one is mellow and resonant, if a little weird.

The chief musical instruments are a form of guitar and a horn, though in worship tambourines, bells and clappers are used.

The Tibetan language is monosyllabic, and it is not difficult for westerners to learn. There are thirty letters in the alphabet, which has been adapted from Sanskrit. Unlike Chinese, it has a system of somewhat complicated verbs. Prefixes and affixes make the written language more difficult. Two kinds of spoken language may be heard—the classical, or that used by the better class, and the simple vernacular of the common people.

There is no education in Tibet as we understand the word, for apart from the lamas, all the knowledge the people have is self-attained. It is said that the lamas try to keep the people in ignorance concerning the outside world. Nevertheless I have been surprised to find that a fair percentage of the population can read—women as well as men.

With regard to home life, Tibetan families are not large, an average number being four or five children. Speaking generally, one son of every family is given to a lamasery to become a lama. He represents his household, and is responsible for the religious rites of the family.

Both polyandry and polygamy are practised all over Tibet, the former being almost universal among the poorer classes, the latter practised by the rich. In the case of polyandry, the several husbands are usually brothers.

The women of Tibet are as a whole respected. In physique they seem as strong as the men, doing as hard and toilsome work as their husbands and brothers. While travelling along the main roads, I have been surprised to meet women carrying heavy loads on their backs, and they are apparently able for it all day. Neither does the man necessarily rule the household in Tibet! When family difficulties arise, husband and wife discuss the situation together, and sometimes the woman makes the final decision.

Although infant mortality is very high, yet for longevity Tibet will bear comparison with other countries. Sad to say, her old people are considered a burden, and they are often so cruelly treated that they die.

The method of attending the sick is very crude, for the Tibetans have little or no knowledge of medicine. Practically all their doctors are from the lama class, and they are considered the wise men of Tibet. They prescribe Chinese medicines almost exclusively. When the doctor is not within reach, the simplest remedies are used, such as rhubarb, liquorice, ginger and other herbal extracts. They are ever at hand, and often efficacious.

Failing cure, the nearest doctor is called. The pulses of both hands are felt for about five minutes each, after which the case is diagnosed. Then the prescription is written and a big fee is asked. Most of the concoctions prescribed are exceedingly bitter, and as they are given in enormous doses, the patient has a very unpleasant time.

For stomach pain of any kind, a good pounding is considered the best form of treatment. The unfortunate victim is made to lie flat on the ground, his gown turned down low from his body. The doctor now takes a small stick and plies it unmercifully on the spot where the pain is greatest, until the patient cries out with anguish. When the outward pain is greater than the inward, cure is claimed.

Teeth are removed by use of stones or hammer and chisel. Unfortunately, two or three other teeth usually come out with the offending one!

In surgical work, the use of the needle is a favourite method. Blood is caused to flow freely by deeply pricking the tips of the fingers. It is interesting to note that the same method is used in dealing with a horse! It is pricked on its tongue, ears, gums, and the tip of its tail, and the treatment often seems to produce the desired effect.

A much practised method for many ailments is that of "cupping", and it is of interest to recollect that this treatment has been used and is still known in western medicine.

A little alcohol is poured into the "cup", and a lighted match is applied. When still aflame, the vessel is "cupped" on to the offending part. The air inside the cup being exhausted, the deeply congested skin is drawn up, the cup held fast. It is left on for about half an hour when relief should come. If blood is to be drawn, the cup is applied to a prepared scarified surface, when the receptacle is quickly filled. The results often appear to be satisfactory.

When the malady is so serious that medical remedies have failed, the lamas are called in to chant their prayers from the sacred books. As there is much wailing and yelling, accompanied by the sounding of bells, cymbals and drums, one would think that the sick man's end would be hastened, but usually he is past knowing what is going on. Sometimes the presiding lama writes prayers on a little slip of paper, and thrusts it down the patient's throat to be swallowed. Leaves of sacred trees are used in the same way. These are pounded to dust, mixed with water, and emptied into the unconscious man's mouth.

The method of disposing of the dead is of gruesome interest. It might be said that there are three modes of process—by air, by fire and by water. The first is the most common way.

The family forms a long procession, and then the lamas, carrying the body, lead the way to some specified sacred hill. On arrival at the summit, the chief lama begins his horrible work. He draws

D

a knife swiftly across the corpse, and then proceeds to sever the flesh in chunks, which he holds out at arm's length. Although at first not a bird may be seen, black eagles quickly appear, and swoop down to seize the flesh. As the lama continues his task, the birds increase in numbers until the sky seems black with them. In a very short time, the greater part of the flesh is disposed of. Now the lama stands aside, and amidst much screeching and fighting, using their powerful talons and hooked beaks, the eagles tear the remainder of the flesh from the skeleton. The lamas now collect the bones which are scattered around, and after pounding them to powder, give it to the carrion birds. Thus every particle of the corpse is devoured.

The black eagle is considered sacred by the Tibetans for this task. It is a large bird, standing about four feet in height, and measuring nine or ten feet from wing to wing. It never attacks a living person. The above ceremony is considered virtuous, and honouring to the dead.

Disposal of a body by fire is, of course, the method of cremation. After the lamas have completed rites similar to those already described, the body is tied up in a cloth and carried by the priests to an open space sacred for the purpose. Fuel is then spread around and over the corpse, and fire is applied. More kindling is added until the body has been fully consumed. The remaining ashes are collected into a small wooden casket, and taken away by the relatives. Should the corpse be that of a lama, the casket is placed in a lamasery for preservation, while if it is that of an Incarnate Buddha, the ashes are put into a *chorten*[1] in the precincts of a lamasery, where they are worshipped for many years to come.

The disposal of the dead by water is similar to the first mentioned process, but instead of the flesh being given to eagles the lama throws it piece by piece into the river, where it is devoured. Is it for this reason that Tibetans will not eat fish?

[1] A tombstone of a Tibetan saint.

CHAPTER IV

RELIGIOUS CONDITIONS

HUMAN hearts the world over yearn for religion! No matter how primitive, unenlightened or degraded a people may be, something must be worshipped and some religious rites be practised. Tibet is no exception.

Up to the seventh century the people of the land had a primitive religion consisting only of witchcraft and sorcery. Shamanism is the name that has been given to it. In or about the year A.D. 639 Buddhism was introduced into Tibet by one named Sbrong-tsan-sgam-po. As in the case of all religious changes, it was not well received. However, it gradually took root, and although it was influenced by the already existing religion in that it embodied spirit-worship and sorcery, it survived and is the state religion of the country to-day. It may also be called Lamaism, that is, Buddhism corrupted by Shamanistic practices and beliefs.

The lamas or priests of Tibet are countless. One son of every family is almost invariably given to a lamasery. He is told that he must renounce all the good things of life and devote himself to a constant round of religious activity. Lamas are the holy men of Tibet. They possess great power, and indirectly become the rulers of the land. They are also believed to have superhuman powers, such as casting out demons, miraculously healing the sick, producing or stopping rain and discovering springs, while the gift of prophecy is also supposed to be theirs.

The name of Gautama, the founder of Buddhism, is unknown among Tibetans. In this district he is spoken of as either Shih-chia-foh or as Sakya Muni, meaning the Precious One. The majority of the people have not the vaguest knowledge of his life and history. If one questions a Tibetan concerning the originator of their religion, one gets only a blank look for answer!

In Tibetan literature there are 108 sacred volumes as well as many others of lesser importance. As in China, all writing is greatly reverenced. Literary works include historical and philosophical treatises, as well as biographies of the sages. Wooden blocks are used almost exclusively for printing, but some books are written laboriously by hand. A big supply of sacred literature, which is greatly prized, is to be found in every lamasery. Many books are printed in gold letters and bound in costly silks.

As well as countless lamaseries, a few nunneries may be found in Tibet. The nuns' dress is similar to that of the lamas, and for this reason it is often difficult to distinguish one from the other. At one time we had a nun staying at our Tibetan Gospel Inn in Sining city, and it was several days before we knew that she was a woman. She had kept her secret from us, as we do not welcome women in the Inn unless accompanied by their husbands or other relations. On the whole, the nuns of Tibet live chaste honourable lives, and they remain in the nunneries till death.

It is interesting to note that Tibetan Buddhism in many ways has a remarkable affinity to Roman Catholicism. Some of the similarities are the rosary, incense, holy water, fasts, processions with mitre and sceptre, acolytes, worship of an image, worship of the saints, pilgrimages and long life retirements. It is thus a simpler matter for a Tibetan Buddhist to become a Roman Catholic than it is for him to embrace Protestant Christianity.

Tibetan Buddhism was reformed during the fifteenth century. The reformer, Tsong K'aba, was born at Sining, and lived in the province of Amdo in the north-east. Legend says that when he was born, not only was he able to speak, but his mental powers were fully developed. In addition, he had long hair and a flowing white beard. At a very early age, he expressed a wish to renounce all worldly ties by becoming a lama. When his mother became aware of his youthful desires, wishing to express her sanction she called for a pair of scissors and therewith cut off his hair, a shorn head being necessary to priesthood. She cast the hair out of the window. On touching the ground it immediately took root, and a beautiful tree sprang up, each leaf of which bore the character for Buddha. This miracle was recognized as a sign from Gautama Buddha that he approved of Tsong K'aba becoming

a lama. The tree is still to be seen in one of the
temple courtyards of Kumbum.

As Tsong K'aba grew up, he showed marvellous
intellectual power, and gained great knowledge.
He built several monasteries and wrote many wise
books. His masterpiece, "The Progressive Path to
Perfection," is a commentary on the sayings of
Gautama Buddha. This work is read and honoured
by all followers of the great reformer.

Tsong K'aba effected the reform while at the
height of his powers. It was followed by a schism,
as the result of which there sprang up a new sect
which took the name of Gelupas, or Yellow caps,
in distinction from the already existing Dukpas, or
Red caps. To-day both sects are much in evidence,
but the one has little to do with the other. They
are easily distinguished by the significant colour of
their entire dress.

Amongst other reforms Tsong K'aba forbade
necromancy, but without success, for it is carried on with
its gruesome results in both sects. He also prohibited
marriage among lamas, and advocated many other
minor reforms. Tsong K'aba has been styled the Luther
of Tibetan Buddhism. According to tradition, he died
in 1478, and his body is preserved in the monastery
of Kaldan not far from Lhassa. It is asserted by
ardent believers who have visited this sacred place
that the corpse is still in a state of fresh preservation,
and that he gives his blessing and speaks words of
comfort to all pilgrims who visit his resting-place.

The Tibetans have been called the most religious
people in the world, and after living among them

one realizes that this statement is not far from the truth. Outwardly, their devotion to religion can be seen at a glance, for every Tibetan carries a number of articles on his person which indicates it. Chief among these may be mentioned the rosary. Old and young, rich and poor, high and low alike are ceaselessly counting their beads, though the word "counting" should rightly be changed to "reading." It is believed that as each of the 108 beads passes through the fingers, the book representing that bead has been read simultaneously. Thus in the space of about one and a half minutes, the whole of the 108 sacred books have been read! In a day, they can be read a few thousand times, for the beads are constantly in use, and the rapidity with which they pass through the fingers is amazing. When not in the hand, the rosary is hung round the neck, but it is not often seen there. I once asked a Tibetan Christian if he missed his beads, and he replied that he was relieved of the burden and duty of continually counting them, but that at first his hands seemed strangely idle and unemployed.

Next in importance to the rosary is the prayer-wheel. This is generally made of either brass, bronze or silver. It is cylindrical in form, and it contains many rolls of paper on which is stamped the Tibetan prayer "Om mani padme hum." The wheel is turned in the hand, always from right to left, and simultaneously the words are muttered innumerable times. Whether at work or leisure, when the rosary is not in use, the wheel is turned during every possible moment. I have seen a Tibetan on horseback at full gallop, one hand holding the reins, the other plying the prayer-wheel. On one occasion, during the whole of a service in Sining, a visiting Tibetan was vigorously turning his prayer-wheel. He was completely oblivious to the smiles of the worshippers, who saw the ludicrous side. To the preacher, it was somewhat distracting.

The words of the prayer formula "om mani padme hum" are now familiar to most people, though I imagine the significance is obscure. Hearing that it had some inner and deeper meaning, and being

"OM MANI PADME HUM"

anxious myself to hear what that meaning was, I once asked my Tibetan teacher to instruct me. He replied that it was impossible to do so just then as it would take him several days.

The generally accepted translation is "Oh thou, the gem in the lotus," an expression of adoration directed to Gautama Buddha, the idea being taken from the fable that Gautama was born from a lotus. The prayer is ever on the lips of all Tibetans. As soon as a child can lisp, he is taught it, and throughout his lifetime until his dying breath, he continues to repeat it. I have often heard it in the abbreviated form of "om mani." The prayer can be seen engraved far and wide on the rocks and stones of the highways; it is written on prayer flags flying in the breeze on shrines at the top of high mountains; it is to be found in lamaseries and tents; I have seen it written on bones suspended from trees, and in every conceivable and inconceivable place. Some even write the words on a stone, and placing it on the ground, walk round it many hundreds of times.

To the Tibetan, the article of paramount importance is his Buddha box. To be without it would certainly mean disaster or calamity. It is suspended by a leathern cord around the neck, and lies on the bare chest. It may differ in size and shape. Usually it is square, though I have seen both oblong and round boxes. Fashioned of either bronze or silver, it varies from about one and a half inches in diameter to four times that size. Within the precious box lies a miniature image of the Buddha. Sometimes printed prayers on yellow paper, and other sacred relics, such as a turquoise stone or the tip of a peacock's feather, are enclosed in the same little casket.

The Tibetan also wears a leather belt to which are attached other religious symbols. Chief of these, fastened to the belt in front, is a miniature bronze casket, oval in shape, which contains an image of Buddha. On either side, at measured intervals, are minute *pulu* bags containing written prayers. Further, numbers of flat bronze Buddhas are attached to the belt. Thus the whole body is encircled with religious mascots, and it is believed that thereby protection is secured, especially while travelling.

The belt finally offers a convenient place for keeping the sword which all Tibetans carry.

As is well known, the highest attainable state to which a Buddhist can aspire is Nirvana, the abode of the perfect. The Tibetan word is "Myang-dia," a literal translation of which is "entire deliverance." "Myang-dia" is a great mystery to all, and although many seek it, very few attain the goal. Those who claim to have reached it have spent long years in meditation and solitude. The object of meditation is to train one's mind to oblivion. To be wholly unconscious of anything, thinking of and caring for nothing, is by no means an easy task, but in order to attain Nirvana, this is necessary. When attained, every passion is in submission, and all sin is supposed to have lost its power.

I have seen a woman in meditation apparently unconscious of all around, her eyes having a vacant stare, her face almost imbecile in expression. When I spoke to her, she took no notice, her eyes although open were as blind, her ears as deaf, and she appeared as if in a trance. I have been told that in order to attain this state, a sure way is to place an image of Buddha before one, and steadfastly to gaze at it until that which is hoped for is attained, the mind unperceiving, sight and hearing lost.

The doctrine of transmigration is firmly believed in by all Tibetans. It was borrowed from Brahmanism in the early stages of Tibetan Buddhism. The states into which souls transmigrate depend on the lives previously lived. The highest attainable is to be a god, while at the other extreme the lowest is to be a demon. The medium course is that of being re-incarnated as a human being. There is an intermediary period between the time of death and re-incarnation, corresponding to the Roman Catholic purgatory. It is believed that unspeakable torments are suffered during this state. Grotesque mural pictures portraying these tortures may be seen in most lamaseries. I recall one which vividly depicted a very energetic demon dragging a massive stone roller over a luckless soul, after which the victim, looking somewhat flat and dejected, was hung over a wall to dry. Endless other forms of torment are painted on monastery walls, reminding one of the old engravings of purgatory by Doré. The intermediate state is believed to last for longer or shorter periods of months or years.

The Tibetan Buddhistic creed includes a Paradise, but it is not so earnestly sought for as might be expected. The hope of re-incarnation in one of the higher states seems to be preferred.

There are thirty-three gods of importance in Tibetan Buddhism, as well as a great number of lesser deities. They are worshipped as idols in lamaseries all over the country.

CHAPTER V

INCARNATE BUDDHAS

NOT only do we constantly meet with Chinese officials, Moslem mullahs[1] and aboriginal chiefs, we also continually come into contact with Tibetan Incarnate Buddhas, often misnamed "living Buddhas." The power of these men is by no means small, for none are higher in rank or more respected than they.

The first Incarnate Buddha, it is alleged, was originally a mere man, but having obtained Nirvana by his uprightness and purity, he was at death promoted to Paradise. But he was not happy in the perfect state, and desired to return to the earth in order to teach men to live so as to obtain Nirvana. His desire was granted, and he became the first re-incarnation of Buddha. From that time to the present day, there have been many thousands of re-incarnations.

On the death of an Incarnate Buddha, how is the new incarnation to be discovered?

When life has ceased, a few male infants who happen to be born about that time are selected. They are carefully watched and guarded until they

[1] A mullah is a Moslem teacher.

reach the age of four or five years, when they are
brought together into one of the lamasery rooms in
which the previous incarnation lived. Before them
are arrayed a number of articles, one of which had
been in the possession of the deceased gentleman.
The little boys are now told to choose one thing which
they would like to have. The fortunate boy who
selects a particular article is believed to be the re-
incarnation, and therewith succeeds to the position
and property which was supposed to have been his
during his former life. One Incarnate Buddha, on
being asked how he was able to discern the right
article, replied, "Why should I not immediately
recognize it, had I not used it for years during my
former sojourn in the world?"

In Sining we have frequent visits from Incarnate
Buddhas, and quite a number have stayed in our
Tibetan Gospel Inn. Some remain for a passing
night only, while others have been our guests for
several consecutive weeks.

I wish for the remainder of this chapter to tell of
our intercourse with two Incarnate Buddhas of
outstanding character. Some of my readers may
know Dr. Susie Rijnhart's book "With the Tibetans
in Tent and Temple," and remember one "Mina
Fuyeh" who lived in the lamasery of Kumbum,
and who came to the assistance of Mr. and Mrs.
Rijnhart during the Mohammedan rebellion of 1895
and 1896. This Incarnate Buddha gave them living
rooms in the lamasery during the several months
of the siege, and thus came into close touch with
missionaries for the first time. In this way, he learned

not a little about Christianity, as well as hearing much of the western world.

A few paragraphs from Dr. Rijnhart's book will be of much service at this point as they describe his personality and character in his earlier years, long before I came into personal touch with him. She writes:—

'Mina Fuyeh was only twenty-seven years old, yet he confidently asserted that he had lived in this palatial abode (Kumbum) previous to the year 1861. He professed even to have vivid recollections of all that pertained to his former incarnation. More than that, he could tell some things that were going to happen in the next! He took great pleasure in prophesying that Mr. Rijnhart would in his next lifetime appear on the earth as a Buddha, as a reward for the good work he was doing in the present existence. . . .

'Soon after we had made his acquaintance, we had given him copies of the Christian Gospels in the Tibetan character, among them a copy of St. John which he prized very highly. He had a marvellous memory, and was soon almost as familiar with the text of the Gospels as we ourselves, and was able quite intelligently to discuss the various incidents in the life of Jesus, quoting passages with extraordinary accuracy and appositeness. He told us that he believed thoroughly in Jesus, but that he did not see any reason why he should renounce Buddhism and become a Christian. He could not see any insurmountable difficulties in accepting both religions, for even on the great doctrine of re-incarnation, with respect to which Christianity and Buddhism are supposed to stand at the opposite poles, he claimed that whereas the Gospels did not explicitly teach the doctrine, yet they did not expressly deny it. He indeed went further and declared his belief that Jesus was no other than a re-incarnation of Buddha, and that Tsong K'aba, the great Tibetan reformer, was a later incarnation of Jesus.

'At the same time, Mina Fuyeh confessed himself charmed with the gospel story. He told us that there were many parallels between Jesus and Tsong K'aba, that the latter had gone about healing the sick and teaching the people just as Jesus had done. When we spoke of the crucifixion, he said that Tsong K'aba had been persecuted too, and added that even to-day in Tibet it was not wise for a lama to be "too good." I believe that, all unconsciously perhaps, Mina Fuyeh has been the means of spreading gospel teaching among his people to an extent that has as yet been possible for no Christian missionary. With all the famous lamas and pilgrims from the far interior, even from Lhassa, as also from Mongolia, he conversed on the subject, telling them what he knew about Christian doctrines, and teaching them to pronounce for the first time the name "Yesu Mashika," Jesus Christ. . . .

'During all our four years' sojourn among the Tibetans of various tribes and districts, we did not meet a single lama who was conversant with even the simple facts of nature. Mina Fuyeh was far above the average, for we found the great mass of them to be ignorant, superstitious and intellectually atrophied like all other priesthoods that have never come in contact with the enlightening and uplifting influence of Christian education. They are living in the dark ages, and are themselves so blind that they are not aware of the darkness. Ten centuries of Buddhism have brought them to their present state of moral and mental stagnation, and it is difficult to believe that any force less than the Gospel of Christ can give them life and progress in the true sense. . . .

'Tibetan lamas would as soon doubt their present existence as question the truth of re-incarnation. With them, it is more than a speculation—it is a fact, the basic postulate of their entire philosophy of life. Mina Fuyeh spoke with the utmost assurance not only of his life-time immediately preceding the present one, but of a score of incarnations through which he had passed since he attained sainthood, and con-cerning each of which his memory stood him in good stead. He was not so far advanced, how-ever, as Sakya Muni (or Gautama), the founder of Buddhism, who, he assured us, was incarnated 551 times, and could remember the 510 incar-nations that preceded his attainment of sainthood as well as the 40 that followed.'

The above paragraphs from Dr. Rijnhart's book give us a very good idea of Mina Fuyeh's interesting

E

personality and broadening religious outlook. My own acquaintance with him dates from about twenty years later, and one visit he paid us stands out especially in my memory.

It was a winter afternoon. Mina Fuyeh was in Sining on business, and before returning to Kumbum, he desired to call on us. Our Chinese servant announced his arrival, and we invited him to our sitting-room. Mina Fuyeh was as usual very cordial and friendly, his chief charm being his naturalness and freedom from constraint and ceremony. For ourselves, it was a great pleasure to have intercourse with one whose interests ranged beyond pasture and cattle. Around a cosy fire and homelike tea-tray—not in Tibetan style—we sat and talked to this charming man on many subjects, chief among them being things pertaining to Christianity. It was evident that he had much knowledge of the Gospel of Jesus Christ, as Dr. Rijnhart testifies.

It was dusk when, accompanied by his servant, he left for Kumbum, a distance of twenty miles. Although they travelled on swift horses they arrived long after dark. The night was bitterly cold, and a big, open charcoal brazier was put into his room. After a hot meal, the curtains were drawn, windows and doors were fastened, and he retired to rest, sinking into a deep sleep after the cold of the night and the fatigue of travelling. In the morning, his servant went to call him but received no response. The door was opened, and Mina Fuyeh was discovered lying still on his bed. They took him out into the open air hoping to revive him, but life was extinct.

MINA FUYEH, THE INCARNATE BUDDHA

This photograph was taken on the very day that he was asphyxiated.

[*Facing page* 66

KURUNG TSERING, THE INCARNATE BUDDHA
The colour of the dress is crimson.

Facing page 67]

The fumes of the charcoal fire had asphyxiated him!

Such was the sudden and tragic end to an honourable life! Of "Yesu Mashika" he knew. He had taught many of his fellow-countrymen to pronounce His name, and he had proclaimed Christian truths to them. But whether he himself believed and trusted in Jesus as his Saviour, only the Great Day will reveal.

The other outstanding character I wish to write of is the most prominent Incarnate Buddha belonging to the red sect in the Koko-nor district. His name is Kurung Tsering. When still a lad in his teens, he left the lamasery and set out on a pilgrimage to Lhassa, a distance of about fifty days' journey. Wishing to accumulate as much merit as possible, he refused to ride an animal, and accomplished part of the journey by prostrating his body at full length on the road, rising, advancing to the spot to which his fingers had reached, and repeating the process *ad infinitum*. On returning from his pilgrimage, he was asked if he had found the peace which he had sought. In reply, he reluctantly admitted that his heart was still void of rest.

Though an Incarnate Buddha, Kurung Tsering has not spent his life in a lamasery. He has a home near the banks of the Yellow River three days' journey from Sining, and in the home, contrary to all Buddhistic precepts, are a wife and children! This fall from celibacy must be explained. When he was still a young man, it was ascertained by necromancy that his present life was his final incarnation, and that after death he would never return to the world again. This caused him much perturbation of mind, and he considered for long how to spend his remaining years. The outcome was that he decided to marry and have a good time!

His wife is a very handsome woman. She is always dressed in costly silks, and her person is adorned with much jewellery. Her black hair is as sheeny as the wings of a raven. It is worn in an enormous plait from which are suspended massive silver ornaments which tinkle and jangle as she walks. She has a winsome personality and a cheery smile for everyone.

The six children with their dark eyes, black hair and ruddy bronze complexions are very attractive in their brightly coloured clothing. The eldest son, Mengpan, was in our Sining Boys' School for some years. He attended daily prayers and the Sunday services along with the other scholars, and thus came into close contact with the Gospel message, but, sad to say, he is far from the Kingdom. The second son is an Incarnate Buddha—a nice lad, and always friendly and pleasant.

Kurung Tsering is a striking personality. His dress is of crimson brocaded satin which is very becoming in contrast to his bronzed complexion. A visit to his home reveals his wealth. A warm welcome always awaits one. Let us look around it! There are assuredly many things to engage our attention. What use has he for a dozen foreign cooking stoves arrayed around his living rooms, we wonder? How can he employ two or three sewing-machines? We notice a galvanic battery, much foreign crockery, and a heterogeneous selection of western furniture. We smile as we see ten or twelve rubber hot water bottles hanging on the walls of his drawing-room. We wonder why he needs so many, and on enquiry, we discover that he does not know for what purpose they were manufactured. He evidently had a more dignified use for them, and seems disappointed when we enlighten him. He shows us his bicycle, and tells us that he is ordering a motor-car, adding that he will not rest content till he owns an aeroplane.

Outside we find a beautiful garden reaching down to the grassy banks of the Yellow River. All kinds of English flowers are growing in it, mostly from seeds I have given him from time to time. Cosmos and sunflowers are seen twelve feet high, and wall-flowers appear as miniature trees. He is passionately fond of his garden, and delights to show its beauty to his friends. Sometimes, however, he gets a little bewildered in the line of demarcation between flowers and vegetables. On one occasion, a fellow missionary was much amused at seeing some splendid cauliflowers growing gloriously in ornamented flowerpots on the terrace.

Kurung Tsering's private temple is near by. It is a most elaborately decorated building both within and without. As we enter, we see costly silken tapestry hangings, while leopard, tiger and wolf skins are spread over seats and divans. Besides possessing this temple, Kurung Tsering presides over about twenty lamaseries, and his district is of no mean size. His wealth is almost untold, and it is added to by his worshippers who never visit him without bringing larger or smaller presents. Offerings of horses, cattle and sheep are brought him in large quantities, while sometimes he receives ingots of silver and gold. In Tibet, an inferior never visits a superior empty-handed.

It is extremely interesting to see one of his subjects come into his presence. Let us watch the procedure! When still at some distance, the inferior starts letting down the long coils of matted hair which are wound round his head. (The members of this religious sect never cut or comb the hair, so that it grows to about ten feet in length.) With bowed body and hair trailing behind, he advances exceedingly slowly. Bowing lower as he proceeds, his body is almost in a kneeling position. During all this time, he keeps his eyes fixed on Kurung Tsering, never lifting them for a single moment. Now he is in his immediate presence, and a look of rapt ecstasy lights up his face. Reverently he produces his scarf of salutation, and with outstretched arms, he places it in both the hands of his superior. He then prostrates himself before him several times, and rising, waits on bended knee for his blessing, which is given by the Incarnate Buddha placing his hand on the worshipper's head. Then with beaming face the suppliant tells his errand, doubts and fears subsiding under the dynamic influence of his chief.

Kurung Tsering often visits Sining and usually stays in the Tibetan Gospel Inn. He is a true gentleman, and we have many times invited him to meals with us in our home. It is interesting to see him skilfully manipulate his knife and fork, which to most Tibetans are considered both cumbersome and unnecessary commodities.

On one occasion when visiting us, he was suffering from toothache and requested me to remove the offending member. Having had much practice in this art at our dispensary, I was only too willing to come to his assistance. Now in Tibet, to see the blood of holy men is not permissible, so the deed had to be performed with the utmost precaution. The windows of our sitting-room were closely curtained, the doors securely bolted, while his private servant kept guard outside. All being in readiness, the operation was successfully carried through, the blood afterwards being buried in the garden under cover of darkness.

In connection with the above incident, I might relate many another entertaining experience, but two or three must suffice.

Once during my earlier years, I was extracting a tooth, when to my horror and confusion, two others came out simultaneously. I evidently appeared much perturbed, for the man smilingly turned to me saying, "It is of no consequence! This will save me having them out on some later occasion!"

Another patient was an old Mohammedan. His tooth was drawn before he realized it. He was delighted, and with a beaming face exclaimed, "I think I will have another out!" I acceded to his request, and he was not satisfied until four others in succession had been removed.

Some years ago, a man came to our mission premises with toothache. He told his complaint to the gatekeeper, who brought me the message. I happened to be hanging pictures in a near-by room. Thoughtlessly I went to speak to the man with a large hammer in my hand, and invited him to the dispensary. His face was indescribable! In spite of explanation, nothing would induce him to trust himself to me, and he made a speedy departure.

Another story concerning the impropriety of common people seeing holy men's blood may be related. Some years ago an Incarnate Buddha was taking a journey to another lamasery. It was in the depth of winter, and while crossing an ice bridge, his horse slipped, causing him to fall heavily to the ground, and inflicting a nasty cut across his eyebrow. The blood flowed freely, and the wound rapidly became swollen and inflamed. Here was a catastrophe! How could he possibly proceed on his way in such a sorry plight? It was unthinkable! The dilemma was solved by the decision to retrace his steps, his retinue with him, and make straight for the Christian missionaries' home, where they were heartily welcomed. His wound was washed and dressings applied. After a good night's rest, the swelling had so much subsided that he was able to return to his private residence. Arriving under cover of darkness, he retired to his sleeping apartment where he secreted himself until his wound was healed. A piece of purple paper was pasted up on the outer door of his residence— a sign denoting that he was unwell. For anyone to enter till it was removed would not only be a breach of etiquette, the wrath of the gods would also descend upon the offender.

To return to Kurung Tsering! It happened a few years ago that nothing was seen of that gentleman! Month after month passed, and still he did not appear. We wondered in vain what had become of him. It seemed as if he had vanished from off the face of the earth. When one encountered his relatives and enquired where he was and how he fared, they would cleverly avoid a reply by changing the subject. But one day the secret leaked out. Kurung Tsering had gone into retirement for a whole year, staying in his own residence, and never leaving his private apartments. When next I met him, he explained his strange action.

"This was my thirty-ninth year," he said, "and my previous incarnations have all died at that age. By keeping to my own dwelling-place, all dangers have been avoided, for I did not wish to leave the world so soon." He is still living!

Kurung Tsering has an adventurous spirit, and advocates travelling for broadening the mind. Some years ago, he took a long-desired trip to Peking, where he was a guest in a Tibetan lamasery belonging to the yellow sect. He had introductions to all the leading officials of the city, who were as interested in seeing him as he them. He even had the honour of being received by the President of China, who was then residing in the ancient capital. He offered the President a present worth thousands of dollars, receiving a costly gift in return. He was treated with all the more honour and ceremony as no Incarnate

Buddha of the red sect had visited Peking for about three hundred years. His three months' sojourn was filled with sight-seeing and engagements, and nothing of any importance was omitted. To hear him tell of his experiences is most entertaining. The thrill and excitement of the 60 m.p.h. car which conveyed him about in sight-seeing is one of his themes. "All you have to do," he told me, "is to sit and hold tight, and keep turning your head from side to side to watch the sights."

Kurung Tsering had never seen the sea before, so he hailed with delight the suggestion of a sail on a private launch down the river from Tientsin to the open sea. During the few hours' journey, he was invited to partake of a tempting menu in the saloon. His realistic story of what followed later when on the open sea is better unwritten. Suffice it to say that he requested to be taken speedily back to land, and that a cherished desire to visit England has waned since his sail in the nearer waters of the China Sea.

Another subject of which he speaks is his attendance at an English Church service. Although he could understand nothing of the strange language, he was profoundly impressed by the reverence of the worshippers and the quietness. The pipe organ, too, seemed very wonderful, and when he was told that it was but a small one, he could hardly credit it. His presence at this service has re-opened the way for more converse on things concerning the Kingdom. He seems halting between two opinions, for neither will he receive Christianity, nor does he oppose it.

As indication of his partial acceptance, I will here insert, with permission, the translation of a letter he wrote to one of my fellow missionaries, the Rev. T. Sörensen:—

"I, your humble servant, have seen several copies of the Scriptures, and having read them carefully, they certainly make me believe in Christ. I understand a little of the outstanding principles, and the doctrinal teaching of the One Son, but as to the Holy Spirit's nature and essence, and as to the origin of this religion, I am not at all clear. It is therefore important that the doctrinal principles of this religion should be explained, so as to enlighten the unintelligent people of small mental ability. The teaching of the science of medicine and astrology is also very important. It is therefore evident if we want this blessing openly manifested, we must believe in the religion of the only Son of God. Being in earnest, I therefore pray you from my heart not to consider this letter lightly. With a hundred salutations."

Enclosed with this letter was a piece of poetry, written in the most elegant language, but which loses much of its beauty in translation. It reads as follows:—

"O Thou supreme God and most precious Father,
    The Truth above all religions,
    The Ruler of all animate and inanimate worlds!
    Greater than wisdom, separated from birth and
        death,
    Is His Son Christ the Lord,

Shining in glory among endless Beings,
Incomprehensible wonder, miraculously made!
In His teaching I myself also believe.
As your spirit is with heaven united,
My soul undivided is seeking the truth,
Jesus the Saviour's desire fulfilling.
For the coming of the Kingdom of Heaven I
    am praying.
Happiness to all!"

What would it mean if a man of Kurung Tsering's position and rank were to renounce Buddhism and embrace Christianity? Would it be either that his thousands of followers became Christian en masse, or would they turn against him and seek his life? Unless he makes the great decision, and surrenders his all to Christ, we cannot say.

Oh, where are the young men from our home countries who will come and share the joy of bringing the Gospel of salvation to such men as Kurung Tsering?

Several months later.

The news has recently been received that he has passed behind the veil. He is greatly mourned by all his devoted followers and many friends, for he was a popular man.

Might not our Lord have said to him, as He did to the scribe of old, "Thou are not far from the Kingdom of God"?

But, alas, as far as we could see, Kurung Tsering did not actually enter through the Door.

CHAPTER VI

IT has been said that the lamaseries of Tibet are the hotbeds of intriguing Tibetan Buddhism, and this is not far from the truth. Scattered throughout the land, there are exceedingly large numbers of these sacred edifices, and they are usually situated in the most beautiful and commanding positions. At the smaller ones may be found twenty or thirty priests, while the larger lamaseries can boast of several hundred or even thousand resident lamas.

Twenty miles south of Sining is located a lamasery of world-wide fame—one already mentioned in this narrative. It contains an unlimited number of idols, and when I say that the Tibetan word "kum" means "ten thousand", while the English equivalent for "bum" is "image," the reader will surmise that it is the monastery of Kumbum to which I am directing attention.

"The lamasery of ten thousand images" is second only in importance and renown to Lhassa, and it draws sightseers from every continent. It is even mentioned in some geography books as being famous for its yearly "Butter Festival." The fact that within its precincts may be found about 3,600 resident lamas gives some idea of its magnitude.

It is my intention to request the reader to accompany me in imagination to this famous lamasery. Travelling by swift horse from Sining, Kumbum can be reached in three hours, though the casual pedestrian takes about a day to cover the distance. As we come over the brow of the last hill—for our journey is a succession of valley and dale and mountain—a wonderful view is spread out before us.

A panorama of turreted temples, with spotlessly white walls, and a roof of glittering gold is what strikes us primarily. One house, however, stands out conspicuously. It is situated high up above the other many buildings, and in contrast to the dazzling white of their walls, this residence is painted bright red. Here lives the great incarnation of Tsong K'aba, the reformer of Tibetan Buddhism. Once a day he is seen to leave his dwelling-place in order to attend the religious ceremony in the famous Prayer Hall. He is accompanied by a number of lamas holding ignited incense. They are clad in bright yellow robes and high cock's comb-crowned mitres of the same hue. The great Incarnation himself is magnificent in the finest yellow brocaded satin with tall yellow mitre. In one hand he holds a golden sceptre, and in the other a priceless rosary of carved ivory and coral. We are struck with the solemnity and splendour, even though it be empty and pagan.

But as we stand and survey the view before us, it is the general whiteness of the walls of the lamasery that stands out most strikingly. Not only those of the chief buildings but of the smaller houses and all boundary walls, as well as the walls of the numerous villas inhabited by the lamas—all appear dazzlingly clean and spotless. One wonders how they are kept so white, but the process is very simple and efficient in Kumbum. Twice a year, huge tanks of white-wash are prepared. A few lamas, pails in hand, climb to the top of a wall and neatly pour the contents over the edge, the whitewash doing its own work by run-ning down the surface of the wall more or less evenly. A second pouring completes the task. Should there be any spot left untouched, a dab with a big brush speedily whitens it.

Adjoining the lamasery on the side of the hill nestles the little market-town of Lusar. It contains several hundred families—for an eastern town is more often numbered by its households than by its individuals. The population of Lusar consists mostly of Moham-medans, though Chinese, Mongols and Tibetans are also represented among its inhabitants. There is a main street which is always a busy sight, for a brisk trade is carried on. This is mostly in the hands of the ubiquitous Moslem, for he is a keen and clever trader wherever he goes.

Lusar monopolizes all the trade of the lamasery, and many kinds of merchandise may be found there. Articles pertaining to religion predominate, and the various paraphernalia for worship—prayer-wheels, drums and bells, rosaries, butter-lamps and idols—are sold in no small quantity. Food shops, too, are there in plenty, for the thousands of lamas feed well.

Although meat is a forbidden article, the butchers have a profitable time selling it to the holy men as well as to the other inhabitants of the little town. Shops selling silk, woollen, and cotton materials display their goods, while homely commodities and household requisites as well as the more tempting brass, silver or bronze ornaments, precious stones and other enticements, are also arrayed. The western traveller revels in the variety of antiques, and he is invariably beguiled into purchasing all manner of curios which will be a delight to him in after years. Foreign firms which purchase sheep's wool from Tibet for export may be found in Lusar too. The wool is carried down on yak or camel back to Sining, where it is put on rafts and floated down the West River which joins the Yellow River, eventually reaching Tientsin, whence it is shipped to foreign countries.

Let us now wend our way towards the lamasery. It is bounded by a circular path, and as we approach, our attention is drawn to a continuous stream of pilgrims who are encircling the sacred enclosure by prostration. Let us stand and watch! Can it be that these are really human beings—men and women, both old and young, as well as children— all on the same intent? What zeal! What exertion! What weariness!

Going down on hands and knees, knocking their foreheads on the ground, stretching their full length on the road, marking their reach with their finger-tips, rising again, toeing the mark in the dust, and wearily repeating the action until the lamasery has been encricled many times—such is the painful

[Photo by T. H. Candlin

The Eight "Chorten" at the Entrance of the Kumbum Lamasery

[Facing page 80

"Bright-eyed, merry-faced boys give us an exuberant welcome."

An old Lama near Sining, said to be ninety years of age.

progress of these pilgrims who come journeys of many days or weeks or even months seeking merit and peace of heart! I remember the great hush that came over me, and the feeling of utter helplessness, the first time I saw these things. Tears welled up in my eyes as I went on my way.

Now we are at the gate of the lamasery. As we enter, we are met by a number of bright-eyed, merry-faced boys who give us an exuberant welcome. They are hatless and we notice their closely-cropped hair —for these boys are lamas in the making. Each one is wearing a long red shawl wound loosely round the shoulders, a *pulu* skirt of the same colour, and big leather boots. Their arms are bare. These little lads are delighted to see us, and they jump and dance around us (for one of us is an old friend), eagerly asking if they can lead us round the monastery. Sad to say, growing up in such an environment, their joyous smiles gradually cease, and their faces become stern and lustreless.

At the entrance of the lamasery we are confronted with eight tombstones known in Tibet as *chorten*. They are simple in design and consist of a succession of tiers on a square base, while they are embellished at the top with a big round ball decorated with a spiral ornament.

Chorten are found at every lamasery, though they vary from about ten to nearly a hundred feet in height. There is one colossal *chorten* in the middle of the road between Kumbum and Lusar which has an archway cut through its base big enough to enable traffic to pass through it. By means of the inevitable

F

whitewash bucket, *chorten* are kept spotlessly clean, and with gold characters in Sanskrit painted on the whiteness, their general effect is very striking. Inside each *chorten* is hidden a reliquary containing the ashes of some sainted lama or Incarnate Buddha.

The story concerning the eight *chorten* at the entrance of the Kumbum lamasery is worth relating. A few hundred years ago, when the Chinese were driving the Tibetans out of the district, after weeks of fighting, the Commander Hung U and his soldiers seized the lamasery, and unmercifully devastated it. Eight Incarnate Buddhas were dragged before the commander, who, with a sardonic smile, said to them, "You being Incarnate Buddhas have prophetic powers, have you not?"

The answer was in the affirmative.

"Well," said he, "can you tell me the day of your death?"

They, fearing treachery, said, "We are going to die to-morrow".

"You are liars!" said he, "you shall die to-day!" And without further parley he had them decapitated, thus showing that he could out-prophesy an Incarnate Buddha. Their bodies were afterwards cremated and the eight *chorten* containing their ashes were erected in their memory. Their position at the entrance to the lamasery affords pilgrims and passers-by an opportunity for worship. As we watch, we notice repeated prostrations before each sacred tombstone in turn, after which the worshipper knocks his head on the four corners of each *chorten*. The very ground on which they are built is considered holy, and anyone riding on horseback must dismount in homage and respect.

A few years ago, a foreign traveller, entirely ignorant of this custom, rode by on his horse. He was immediately pounced upon by numberless lamas, who seemed to appear suddenly from nowhere, and dragged him from his steed. He pleaded absolute ignorance, and was eventually allowed to go on his way, but it was a miracle that he escaped with his life.

Of the lamasery buildings, one of the first we enter is the kitchen. This will strike you very uninvitingly as it is but dimly lit. There is only diminutive window space, and the huge iron doors are always kept shut. Immediately opposite the doors, we see many hundreds of *khata* suspended on a wooden frame, looking much like washing hanging out to dry. As usual they are blue or white, but owing to the continual smoke from the open grate, they appear dingy and uncertain in colour. Why this strange array? All pilgrims visiting the lamasery offer a *khata* to the kitchen god as a salutation. The attending lama receives it from the visitor and hangs it on the frame.

Around the kitchen we see shelves on which are kept the buckets for serving food to the lamas. It is a pleasure to observe that the buckets are bright and clean. We next notice three massive cauldrons, each of which has capacity for feeding several hundred lamas. The cauldrons are about ten feet in diameter, and deep enough for a boy to stand up inside. They are made of bronze, and on the outer surface are prayers engraved in Tibetan character. These enormous cauldrons are constantly in use. Once a day the lamas have a meal of vermicelli which is cooked in them. The chief use of the cauldrons, however, is for brewing tea, of which all Tibetans drink copious quantities. *Tsamba* is also made with the tea and is a daily food of the lamas.

The fuel used in cooking is straw, and immense quantities of it are daily required. How is it obtained? It is brought in payment of taxes by those who hold land from the monastery. Grain is likewise demanded in taxation, and the lamasery is maintained in this way. Wide tracts of land are owned, thus bringing in great wealth to the institution.

Leaving the kitchen and turning up a lane to the right, we come to the famous Golden Roof Temple, without doubt the central edifice of the whole lamasery. It is built on a steep slope, and has a commanding position, being visible from almost every part of the grounds. It was erected in memory of the reformer Tsong K'aba, and pilgrims are drawn to it from all over the land. Its roof is covered with pure gold, said to be one eighth of an inch in thickness. When the sun is shining on it, it looks like a blazing fire. Many attempts have been made to capture this temple, but all have failed. Nothing but death would dislodge the lamas, who would fight like tigers in defence of their precious golden roof.

Why this costly and magnificent edifice? It was built to contain a huge image of Tsong K'aba—an idol fashioned of plated gold fifty feet in height. Pilgrims deem themselves unworthy to worship in

his immediate presence, and so perform their prostrations in a certain place outside the temple. This
spot is floored with a specially hard wood, but you
will notice deep grooves in the polished boards.
These are caused by the ceaseless slidings of the
pilgrims' hands and knees in kowtowing. There is
space for ten worshippers at one time. I have been
told that the boards of this floor must be changed
every few months, for with the endless prostrations,
they wear away. How earnest the pilgrims are!
If devotees of a dead Buddha are so sincere, how
much more fervent should we be who adore a living
Christ!

The temple is but dimly lighted with butter lamps
which are kept ever burning before the image. We
can discern many passages leading to different parts
of the interior, and as we grope our way through
them, we see that they are flanked with idol cases
containing some of the "ten thousand images."

Let us now imagine that we are standing in front
of the idol on one of the two great feast days when
it is unveiled—for apart from these two days in the
year, the fifteenth of the first moon, and the sixth of
the sixth moon, the great image is always curtained from
view. The lower part of the idol is lighted by means
of the butter lamps, but as we wish to see its features
better, we will mount some stairs at the side of the
temple leading to a gallery which is level with its
head.

He is in a sitting position with hands outstretched
in the attitude of blessing his worshippers, and in
contrast with the hideousness and repulsiveness of

many idols, Tsong K'aba has a pleasing countenance. Before him on the floor beneath we notice many things arrayed on benches. There are smaller idols, peacocks' feathers, *khata*, prayer bells, trumpets, etc., as well as food offerings of butter, fruit bread, and cakes. A continual stream of people is coming and going, all muttering prayers and knocking their heads on the bench in front of the idol. Standing there silently apart, and looking down on the scene, our hearts are rent at the sadness and pathos of it. "Their idols are silver and gold, the work of men's hands. They have mouths, but they speak not: eyes have they, but they see not: they have ears, but they hear not: noses have they, but they smell not: they have hands, but they handle not: feet have they, but they walk not: neither speak they through their throat. They that make them are like unto them; so is every one that trusteth in them."

Had the Psalmist seen such an image as this, we wonder? Had he watched worshippers such as we see below us with their unshaken loyalty, their unflagging zeal, their unwearied patience, and their ceaseless prostrations? We are overwhelmingly conscious of our own powerlessness, yet we can only offer our poor service afresh to God, crying out in sorrow and longing for the "more labourers" to help bring in the harvest from Tibet.

Directly in front of the temple stands a big sacred tree. It is a species of syringa, and is the one which is claimed to have sprung up from the shorn locks of the boy Tsong K'aba. It is asserted by all devotees of Lamaism that each leaf of the tree bears a hiero-

[*Photo by* F. Doggett Learne*]

THE SACRED SYRINGA AT KUMBUM

The tree is said to have sprung from the shorn hair of Tsong K'aba.

[*Photos by F. Doggett Learner*

Above   Encircling the Lamasery at Kumbum by Prostration
Below : Prayer Wheels at the Lamasery of Koh-mang-sï

Facing page 87]

glyphic for the word "Buddha." We are standing now beneath the tree. A lama is beside us. We notice the leaves are falling in the cool breeze. As they flutter to the ground, the lama is picking them up and placing them in a little wooden box, first examining each leaf carefully.

"Friend," I say to him, "why do you not gather the leaves from the tree rather than waiting for them to fall?"

"That would be a great sin," he replies, "for no one is allowed to pluck them. As the wind blows they fall of themselves, and then only is it permitted for me to touch them."

"And why do you look so carefully at each leaf?" I further ask.

"Do you not know," said he, "that on every leaf there is a character for Buddha?"

"Is there indeed?" I replied. "Will you allow me to see it?"

He thereupon takes a leaf carefully from his box, and hands it to me. I examine minutely but can decipher no writing. The lama is eagerly watching my face.

"Can you not discern it?" he asks.

"No, I see nothing!" I reply.

Thereupon with a look of scorn, he exclaims, "Then surely you are not a believer, for only believers can see!"

We afterwards learn that the leaves are sold to pilgrims for medicinal purposes. They are pounded to dust, stirred with water, and drunk. The mixture is claimed to be a cure for any disease!

Leaving the temple courtyard, we next arrive at the Prayer Hall, which in magnificence of colouring and decoration surpasses the Golden Roof Temple. Surely paint-pots of every possible shade must have been at work here! And yet there seems no clashing of colours, for all seem to blend in harmony with the strangely daring scheme. Column after column supports the overhanging roof of the verandah. Golden dragons on a scarlet ground wind their way gracefully round each pillar, tints of emerald and turquoise introduced here and there. Eaves are resplendent both in design and colour, while the roof consists of decorated tiles in gold, green and blue. Wonderful architecture, and still more wonderful ornamentation!

The doors of the Prayer Hall are handsome specimens of hammered brass. As we stand and look through them, we are awed by the sight of the magnificence within. Silk brocades are hanging from the roof, while beautiful tapestries adorn the pillars. On the walls, we see exquisitely embroidered pictures, all of a religious nature. We wish that there were more light to show up the splendour.

Do you ask me when and how this magnificent Hall is used? It is here that the lamas meet for worship two or three times daily. Let us be spectators during one of their sessions! We must take off our shoes before we enter the building, and we see hundreds of pairs of the lamas' boots in a jumbled mass in the courtyard. It is a wonder to me, their boots all being alike, how ever they recognize their own footgear after worship. Yet I am told that the boots are seldom lost or wrongly claimed.

We walk softly into the Hall in our stockinged feet. The lamas dressed in their prayer clothes are sitting tailor-fashion in long rows on padded mats, facing the central aisle. Loose leaves of a sacred book are now distributed to the worshippers, who are soon engaged in the perusal of the pages, chanting and reciting from them in as big a voice as possible, each one seemingly trying to drown his neighbour's. This chanting is full of that curious eerie melancholy which is peculiar to the East. We notice that the lamas are by no means unconscious of what is going on around them, for although we are moving round quietly that we may not disturb, all eyes are directed towards us.

At the head of the Hall, seated on a decorated throne, is the presiding Incarnate Buddha. From time to time, he leads the lamas in their devotions. In a clear and extraordinarily deep bass voice he chants a sentence, the lamas in concert repeating it after him. This continues for some considerable time, and there can be no slackness, for the eagle eyes of the Incarnate Buddha are on his flock, and none can escape. Should any shirk his duty, a few lashes with a long leathern whip may do serious damage.

The monotony of the long prayers is relieved by the clapping of hands and waving of arms, while the bodies of the lamas sway to and fro rhythmically. Eerie yells punctuate the chanting. A little later, large sea-shells or conches with holes bored in their ends are distributed. These when vigorously blown produce a weird, dull, trumpet-like sound. Long horns are next produced from which issue forth notes strange and deep. Ringing of bells, beating of drums, rattling of bones and clanging of cymbals add to the variety of the programme. Sometimes all the instruments are played in chorus, resulting in a hideous din.

Holy water is sprinkled at intervals on the worshippers, and as the session is rigorous and of long duration, copious quantities of hot tea, with oil cakes and barley flour, are served. These are kept till a given signal and then speedily devoured.

Devotions are now over. Amidst a deep hush, the Incarnate Buddha rises, while all attention is riveted on him. He walks with becoming dignity under a huge yellow and red silk umbrella carried for him by several lamas who escort him down the aisle of the Prayer Hall, through its massive doors and on to his residence in another part of the lamasery grounds. The concluding voluntary is of trumpet blasts and cymbal clangs, during which the worshipful lamas file out in order to the open courtyard where they scramble for their boots in a less orderly manner. Once free in the open air, they behave like children just let out of school! Such a noise! Such shouting and chattering! Such scamperings!

On certain days, the new-comers among the lamas assemble in the courtyard to receive instruction in worship. The Incarnate Buddha's absence is marked by free behaviour and irreverence. Sitting

in long rows on their mats, the youths remind us
of naughty boys, while the priests in charge are like
inefficient schoolmasters unable to discipline their
pupils. One young wit says something funny, another
makes a grimace, and peals of laughter follow.

Once when I was visiting a lamasery, a young
lama was sitting apart in the corner of the courtyard chanting at the top of his voice from his
sacred pages. I ventured to offer him a tract which
he willingly accepted and actually substituted for his
prescribed portion!

We have had many opportunities for present-
ing the Gospel to the lamas of Kumbum. In visiting
their houses, Bible pictures may be seen on the walls
of their rooms, and Christian literature among their
sacred books. Thus the seed is being sown, but only
when the Great Harvest is gathered in shall we
know what has been reaped from Kumbum.

We must not leave the lamasery grounds without
visiting the Museum, a small building containing
a variety of articles and sacred relics. Many specimens of stuffed wild animals are among the exhibits
and never fail to attract visitors. Musical instruments, ancient and modern, are on show, and are
of special interest to the western traveller. In the
upper story are many idols before which all pilgrims
place offerings. One idol in particular is sure of
a visit from Easterners and Westerners alike. It
is the image of a renowned Incarnate Buddha. The
legend concerning this idol is of quaint interest.
When it was moulded some hundreds of years ago,
the model was scarcely completed when hair appeared

on the head and has continued growing until it
reached the length that it is to-day! For purposes
of preservation, it is kept in a glass case, and pilgrims
are thus prevented from handling it.

Another relic which is greatly prized by the lamasery is a picture of Tsong K'aba. The story regarding
it is as follows. While as a lad the reformer was a
student in Lhassa, he wished to send his mother a
present, for she, as previously related, lived in the
far side of Tibet. He therefore drew a picture of
himself, using his own blood in place of ink, and
sent it to her by returning pilgrims. This is preserved
in the Museum.

We have now visited the principal buildings of
Kumbum, and as we have walked from one to the
other, I am sure you will have noticed many strange-
looking cylinders standing in every possible corner
of the lamasery grounds. Let me tell you that they
are fixed prayer-wheels. (It will be remembered
that the nomad Tibetan always carries a tiny prayer-
wheel in the voluminous folds of his pocket.) The
fixed wheels vary from about one foot to twelve in
height. The cylinders contain long strips of paper
which are printed all over with the one same prayer
—"om mani padme hum"—and wound tightly
round the axle of the wheel.

Starting from a certain spot, pilgrims make a
tour of the lamasery grounds to "do" the prayer-
wheels. The journey is always from right to left to
avoid collision with other worshippers. A vigorous
push sends a wheel spinning round on its pivot.
It is believed that the prayer is repeated once for

every revolution, and as there are several hundreds of the wheels, a large accumulation of merit can be acquired in a comparatively short time.

Two giant wheels occupy little houses each to itself. They are very heavy, as they contain hundreds of yards of prayer paper, and so require great strength to set going. When revolving, they can be heard from a considerable distance. Although butter is so plentiful, it is used sparingly as a lubricant, and the squeaking and groaning of these two prayer-wheels are apt to set one's nerves on edge.

Now at last we will take our departure from the lamasery. But, before leaving the neighbourhood, I want to conduct you on a short pilgrimage to a sacred mountain behind Lusar. Rising at dawn, we make our way through the streets of the little town. Although at so early an hour, everyone is astir, and some are already making their way to the foot of the mountain. We notice that packets of coloured paper, sticks of incense and bundles of firewood are being carried. We ascend the mountain path along with many others who all appear bent on some purpose. For what reason are they going up the mountain so early, and why are they so intent? At the summit is a shrine where they are going to worship.

About half way up, we suddenly see a man fall full length face downwards on the mountain side, his head towards the summit. He knocks his fore-head on the ground, and then he rises and repeats a similar process on the same spot. A third and fourth repetition do not satisfy him. He is going to perform this kowtow maybe several hundred times before he believes himself worthy to ascend higher.

On arrival at the summit, we see many pilgrims already at their worship. They are burning incense as well as fragrant branches of pine and cedar wood at an altar in a miniature temple. Grain is also offered at the shrine.

Near by is a large bronze bell under a wooden canopy. It is sounded by all pilgrims in order to direct the attention of the idol in the shrine to the offerings placed before it. Columns of blue smoke are ascending to heaven from the burning sacrifices.

Your attention is next attracted by tiny pieces of paper floating around here and there in the breeze. Wonderingly you see a pilgrim taking a handful of yellow, white and red leaflets from his wallet. After repeating a prayer, he holds them high up over his head, and then as he opens his hand the wind carries them from him, most of them fluttering and flying away like enormous butterflies. On picking one up you see that it bears a tiny picture of a horse, and then you discover that all the leaves have the same picture printed on them. You look at me askance and I enlighten you by explaining that the pilgrims believe that when a "wind horse" falls to the ground at some weary traveller's feet, it takes life. Thus the footsore wayfarer is able to ride to his journey's end. The idea is a quaint one and would be a good subject for a pretty fairy story. The pilgrim's motive in this act is not so much that of kindness as that of obtaining merit—a motive which is behind so many of their other deeds.

We wend our way down the mountain with mingled feelings of interest, pity and longing. The temple roofs and minarets and white-washed walls of Kumbum are before us, the Golden Roof blazing in the midday sun. "Go ye . . . and preach the Gospel," said our Lord, and many have obeyed His command. The Good News *has* been proclaimed in the lamasery of Kumbum. Systematic visits have been made by missionaries and colporteurs alike. Friendliness and confidence have been gained among the lamas and even among the Incarnate Buddhas.

A wonder? Yes! But Christ said, "Thou shalt see greater things than these."

A TIBETAN "WIND HORSE"
(*Facsimile*)

CHAPTER VII

TWO KUMBUM FESTIVALS

You will remember that twice a year the enormous golden image of Tsong K'aba is unveiled in the Golden Roof Temple. These are two great days for Kumbum, and I wish again to invite my reader to accompany me to both celebrations.

The one which is called "The Buddha-Airing Festival" must of necessity take place in summer weather, for it is held in the open air, so the sixth day of the sixth moon is a very suitable date for it. Strangely enough it has scarcely ever been known to rain in Kumbum on that day.

Had we explored a dark recess at the back of the Golden Roof Temple, we might have seen a mysterious long canvas roll, and wondered what it could possibly contain. We need not wonder longer, for to-day it is coming out for its annual "airing!"

For many hours beforehand much chanting may be heard in preparation, after which, at a specified signal, the stupendous roll is hoisted on to the shoulders of twenty stalwart lamas by whom it is borne towards a hill just outside the lamasery grounds. Watched from a distance, it looks extraordinarily like a gigantic caterpillar meandering up the hillside.

On its arrival at the appointed location, the burden is placed reverently on the grassy slope and the lamas proceed to unroll it. Around us are immense crowds of people, for Tibetans and Mongols alike, as well as Chinese, have assembled to worship a silken Buddha. Amidst much chanting and reciting of prayers, with a heavy aroma of incense, and to the accompaniment of drums, horns, bugles and cymbals, a veritable masterpiece of silken embroidery is unfolded. The Buddha is represented in the attitude of receiving his worshippers. In one hand he holds a religious emblem while the other is raised high in blessing. Around him are various Buddhistic symbols and lesser gods. The embroidery is amazingly beautiful, and as the sun shines down gloriously upon it, it seems that every colour conceivable must have been woven in. I think I hear you exclaim that you have never seen anything so exquisitely beautiful before!

Let us now turn our attention to the worshippers. Amidst the deafening blare of the unmusical instruments, the many thousands of people are prostrating themselves unceasingly. In the kowtowings which you witnessed outside the Golden Roof Temple, Tsong K'aba was the object of worship, but this silken masterpiece of embroidery represents the Buddha himself, and it is before this symbol of him that the multitude falls down in adoration.

But something else catches your attention. People seem to be crawling on the ground from beneath the huge sheet! You are watching with rapt gaze. What can it mean? You perceive that the canvas does not rest on the ground, as it appears in the distance to do, but is stretched about three feet above it. Coming nearer, you observe that the people who emerge from beneath the sheet are sick and diseased. It is with a sad heart that I explain to you that these poor sick folk believe that any physical ailment may be cured by passing beneath the Buddha from one side to the other. So it is that the maimed and the halt and the blind gather together on this great day, and as they crawl painfully and laboriously under the sheet, they hope to be cured of their diseases when they emerge on the other side. As we watch the pathetic sight, our minds go back to the time of our Lord, and we remember the joy of the infirm, the lame, the leper, the mentally afflicted and the dying, who at His touch were made perfectly whole. And here are these sick and suffering ones seeking relief by wriggling on all fours under a piece of embroidery! A wave of helpless pity sweeps over us! "Lord, how long?"

The other great day in the calendar of Kumbum is the fifteenth of the first moon. It is called the "Festival of Flowers," though there are certainly no flowers visible in the depths of a Tibetan winter! More usually, it is spoken of as the "Butter-God Festival"—a fitting appellation, as you will agree when you behold it with me.

The crowds that gather together for this great occasion are enormous, and unlike the "Buddha-Airing Festival," to which worshippers come mainly from the vicinity, pilgrims assemble for the gaieties and worship of the fifteenth of the first moon from

THE "BUDDHA-AIRING" FESTIVAL AT KUMBUM   [*Photo by T. H. Candlin*

[Photo by J. T. Mathewson

A MINIATURE BUTTER IMAGE AT THE KUMBUM FESTIVAL

both near and far—some even travelling from Lhassa itself.

For a few days before the festival, all roads leading to Kumbum are filled with pilgrims. They come from north, south, east and west, travelling on horse, mule, donkey, yak or camel. No distance is too great to prevent the pilgrim from attending this celebration, no hardship too irksome, no weather too severe. He cannot be turned from his purpose and his enthusiasm cannot be quenched.

In addition to the pilgrims who journey on animal back, hundreds of pedestrians—if such they may be called—travel to Kumbum covering the ground by prostration. What pitiable objects to behold! They are dressed in sheepskin gowns, the woolly sides next their bodies becoming vermin-infested, and the outer side caked with mud and dust as they travel. Often they journey several weeks or months in this way. In their hands they hold pieces of wood to protect the skin from being torn on the stony roads, while their knees are bound with leather. What wretched specimens of humanity! It is hard to realize at first glance that they actually are human beings, covered with dirt and mud, and begrimed from head to foot as they are! Much more degraded by far do they appear than the lordly camel and handsome yak which thread their way among them as they grovel on the dusty road!

Let us first visit the bazaar outside the lamasery. The thousands of pilgrims assembling in Kumbum for this season offer too good a chance for tradesmen to miss. From Sining and other large towns they bring their wares, setting up stalls at the side of the main road, while the more prosperous merchants erect pavilions of white calico in which to array their goods. A flourishing trade is carried on. Rich and poor, high and low are there, jostling and elbowing each other as they bargain over the tempting wares.

Everyone is dressed in new and brightly coloured clothes, whether of costly silks, comfortable *pulus*, or homely cotton materials, and all spend money lavishly. Purchasers move briskly from stall to stall, making a kaleidoscopic effect of colour. Silks and cotton materials and *pulus* are without doubt the merchandise most in demand, the best sellers being scarlet, royal blue, emerald and orange—the favourite colours of all Tibetans and Mongols. A variety of nicknackery may be seen on other stalls. Here are brass idols, Buddha boxes, peacocks' feathers, jade stones and butter bowls. Here are medicines, tobacco, tea and incense, while sugar-candy, sultanas and other sweetmeats and dainties occupy another stall.

Pedlars too there are who catcall up and down the streets advertising their goods—squeaking dolls, chirping birds and jumping dogs—reminding me (with a twitch at my heartstrings!) of Cheapside at the Christmas season. Here is a Tibetan with a leopard skin slung across his shoulder, here another holding out a bunch of magnificent peacocks' feathers, and now we are accosted by a man offering us a string of turquoises. All are shouting their lustiest and adding their London-like street cries to the general hullabaloo, to such an extent that we are glad to escape!

But in the hustling, bustling streets of the bazaar may be seen one stall which is different from all the others—none other than our own book-stall from Sining with Tibetan evangelist, Chinese colporteur and missionary all busily at work. For if the traders from other towns find the Kumbum festivals a good opportunity to sell their wares, we heralds of the Gospel also consider it too great a chance to miss. So we go up some days beforehand, and as the pilgrims begin to arrive from the far-off places, we are there with the Word of God in readiness for them. We set up our stall in the heart of the bazaar, and as the strangely assorted crowd moves along, we publish both in Tibetan and in Chinese the Name which is above every name. We also sell thousands of gospels as well as distributing picture leaflets and tracts as we move in and out among the multitude. Who knows to what remote homesteads and encampments these books and leaflets may travel?

On the day before the Butter Festival, a performance called the "Devil Dance" is held. It is well worth a visit, for it is considered an important part of Buddhistic religious festivities. Performed in the huge courtyard outside the Prayer Hall, it is attended by many hundreds of the pilgrims who assemble for the Butter Festival.

From early in the morning spectators begin to take their places, until at midday every available corner is occupied, space being left only in the centre for the performers. On the south side, high up on a wooden platform, the band takes its place. Do you picture it as consisting of trombones, cornets, flutes, etc.? Would that it did! Three instruments only are used—cymbals, drums and bugles—and the "music" may be described as a deafening din, though at times, to harmonize with the dancing, it calms down considerably. The dancers take all their directions from this band. On the opposite side of the spacious courtyard a temporary throne is erected for the great Incarnation of Tsong K'aba, who attends in state.

By noon all is in readiness. The performers are dressed in their costumes, the Incarnate Buddha resplendent in gorgeous array is seated on his throne, the enormous audience is eagerly expectant, and the band only requires the signal to begin.

The Devil Dance is divided into several sections. Let us watch them one by one. First appear four young lama boys who are dressed to represent four demons. To the accompaniment of the band they move forward to the centre of the courtyard, and there perform a simple dance, their object apparently being to show their skill in balancing on each foot in turn, while poising the other high in the air. After about ten minutes of graceful movements, they retire as they came in, and our opinion is that there is nothing very devilish in that item.

Immediately after their exit, six individuals come into the arena wearing dresses of handsome blue and green brocaded satins decorated with ivory ornaments. They are disguised with huge baby-faced masks giving a peculiar and somewhat uncanny effect. Nothing of any note marks their dancing, and as

DEVIL DANCERS AT KUMBUM

THE KUMBUM LAMASERY

Only about a quarter of the whole lamasery appears in this picture.

they continue it for some considerable time, we are
inclined to think that we have come to a rather
inferior show.

On their departure six grotesque figures, to a
vigorous band accompaniment, dash wildly to their
positions in the centre of the courtyard. They are
dressed in white, yellow and red. Three of them are
disguised with huge masks representing yak, while
the other three are hooded with deer heads. In their
right hands they carry swords which they brandish
fiercely while they go through their wild masquerade.
The dance is too strenuous to keep up long, and they
soon make an exit as fantastic as their entrance, the
three deer preceding the yak.

While we are still blinking our eyes and taking
breath, the six baby-faced actors appear carrying a
huge rug which they spread on the ground in front
of the Incarnate Buddha. Behind them enter the
four boy lama demons. As they are dancing in the
centre of the arena, another lama appears carrying
an image on a tray, and while the demon boys are
elegantly ambling around the rug, the lama puts
the tray down upon it. He also places a chair in
front of the carpet. The next actor is a very old
woman who advances and seats herself on the vacant
chair. Her movements are so slow that we have
time to note her exquisite gold-embroidered robe
which glistens in the sun.

At this point two trumpeters proceed into the arena,
heralding the approach of the central figure of the
whole entertainment. He is elaborately dressed in
various colours, but our attention is taken up with

the grotesqueness of his head. It is an enormous
mask of black and gold with horrible eyes and huge
horns. In one hand he carries a human skull. We
are told that he is the god of sickness and death, and
we shudder as we watch him. All the eyes of the
hundreds of worshippers are riveted on him and we
note a look of abject fear on the faces around us.
Some even seem to tremble at his presence. Various
individuals from the crowd come forward and offer
this monstrosity scarves of salutation, which are
received for him and hung on to his back by two
attendants. Recovery from sickness or disease is
hoped for by this act. The ghastly individual now
sways and dances slowly around, the band playing
eerie uncanny music, until the appearance of about
twenty-five other figures who follow each other into
the arena. They wear three-eyed devil heads of
different colours, and there is a skull painted on the
forehead of each mask. Their clothes are of gorgeous
multi-coloured silks.

Now the six yak and deer-head actors enter again,
and by this time there are nearly fifty players on the
stage. They go through an exhibition of weird
dancing, and were it not for the heathenish atmosphere
and the devil faces which fill us with awe, the spec-
tacular effect would be extraordinarily picturesque
and magnificent.

While they continue their measured movements, the
rug with the image upon it is removed to the centre
of the courtyard and the actors form a huge circle
around it. Suddenly every figure stops and remains
lifelessly still, the music almost dying away. Then

the three deer performers abruptly leave the circle, and amidst clangings and clashings of the band, go through a short but violent dance, concluding by placing themselves in front of the rug. Breathlessly we watch the whole circle kneel on the ground, and in silence the god of sickness and death takes a knife and decapitates the image on the tray, throwing it from him at random among the crowd.

Thus ends this extraordinary exhibition, and the bizarre actors slowly dance their exit. When all have left the arena the Incarnate Buddha is escorted with pomp from the courtyard and the crowd disperses.

We leave in a state of bewilderment. Have we been dreaming or have we witnessed reality? We know that the impression stamped upon our minds will never be effaced, while the superstition and heathenism revealed in the performance make us sick at heart.

We awake on the morning of the fifteenth of the first moon to a day of blue sky and keen frosty air. We spend some hours with our evangelists among the crowds around the lamasery or at our bookstall, and then, as evening falls, we watch the sun like a ball of fire disappear behind the snow-covered mountains which become ablaze with orange and gold, rose and purple. Afterwards in the darkening sky the full moon rises—for on the fifteenth of every Chinese month the moon is "round"—and there is anticipation in the air, as well as frost, for the great Butter Festival is about to begin, and the thousands of pilgrims are agog with excitement.

For many weeks beforehand about thirty-five of the lamas have been at work in the back premises of the lamasery moulding the butter images in readiness for the great occasion, and, the work complete, to-day they have been brought out and put in position, each one in its appointed place. In all, about thirty large butter idols have been modelled, as well as innumerable smaller figures which are used as ornamentation around the bigger pieces.

Platforms have been erected in readiness for the idols, of which all but two are placed at intervals in the temple yards or open spaces of the lamasery grounds. The two remaining images, however, are much bigger than the rest, and during the day two "Pavilions of Silk" have been prepared for them. The framework of these pavilions is of the boughs of pine trees, lashed together with stout ropes. This scaffolding is covered with silken tapestries exquisitely embroidered. These all face inwards and are hung close together forming the walls of the pavilions. The tapestries are all of a religious nature representing the gods of Tibetan Buddhism. Every imaginable colour is used in the embroideries though blue seems to predominate.

All the images, whether the two masterpieces in the Pavilions of Silk or those in the open spaces of the lamasery, represent Buddha. They vary little in form except in the decorations around them. In every case the Buddha is in a sitting position. One hand is holding a religious symbol, the other is raised aloft as if blessing his worshippers. He is arrayed in beautiful robes of soft colours all blending in harmony. His face bears a placid smile as though gratified with the homage rendered to him. The colour of his flesh is true to life. Very wonderful it is to think that these butter images are modelled by hand—so realistic are both features and raiment. More wonderful than all, however, are the crowns on the heads of the gods. It seems scarcely possible that the fine filigree work is not real gold, and that the dazzling jewels—rubies, sapphires, opals, amethysts and emeralds—are not actual precious stones. And yet from the tip of the crown to the hem of the silken robes, every scrap of the images is nothing but Tibetan butter! One's mind goes back to the extraordinarily fascinating and realistic array of wax figures in Madame Tussaud's, and yet, for sheer ingenuity, these images moulded by the hands of Tibetans, and all—faces, hands, clothes and crowns—all of butter, are surely unrivalled!

As decoration around each central image, innumerable minute figures are arrayed. Here are horses, deer, elephants, mice, dogs, snakes, etc., each life-like in colour. Here are castles with battlement walls. Here are beautiful flowers intertwined, the lovely lotus especially prominent. Here are terribly real battle scenes. Horse-soldiers are advancing as the enemy falls back. Bellowing cannons are seen pouring forth their shot. The ground is strewn with the dead. Here are houses, lamaseries and tents. Here are realistic scenes from hell and paradise, and here is an enormous dragon slithering in and out among the miniature figures around the butter god. Every scale of his green slimy body is

visible. His tail is raised high in the air as if about
to lash in fury. His fearsome head is poised in readiness for attack, his eyes standing out with rage, his
huge open mouth and sharp fangs ready to devour
his prey. His claws almost make one shudder. And
the wonder of it comes over us again—*butter*!

But what of the masses of pilgrims who have now
assembled and who remind us of the swarming of
bees? How are they to be controlled? From Sining
the Mohammedan General has sent up 3,000 soldiers
to be in readiness. They camp out on the hills round
about Kumbum and are largely responsible for the
good order of the crowds.

Within the lamasery, too, many of the taller and
more stalwart lamas are appointed for the evening
to maintain control. These "black lamas," as they
are called because of their blackened faces, are
armed with long leathern whips, and if the multitude
becomes unruly they lash out unmercifully to regain
order.

But the crowd is moving! Let us stand aside and
watch. The scene is lit up by hundreds and hundreds
of little butter lamps, three tiers being placed at the
foot of each image. The lamps are small brass
bowls filled with the liquid butter, a wick floating in
each. Lama boys with large pitchers of liquid fat
are put on duty, and they replenish the bowls as
required. The lamps are so efficient that worshippers
can see the minutest details at the different shrines.

About two hours must be spent in going the round
of the images, the soldiers and "black lamas"
regulating the pilgrimage, which is all in one direc-

tion. Here all classes are levelled. All sorts and conditions of men are united in a common purpose —worshipping gods of butter! The rich Lhassa merchant, the poor dust-begrimed pilgrim, the Incarnate Buddha in all his finery, the nomad in his simple gown of sheepskin, the Mongol Prince with his retinue of beautiful princesses, the humble tent-dweller, the aboriginal chief—all closely packed together regardless of position or rank—whether Chinese, Mongols, Tibetans, Moslems or aboriginals —all passing in a continuous stream before the butter images. Listen to the murmur of their prayers! Watch their hurried prostrations! What eagerness and adoration on their faces as they enter the silk pavilions and bow down! Beside one of these masterpieces, which is about four times the size of life, is a smaller god which nods its head as if in acknowledgment of the prostrations. A small lama boy is hidden at the back of the pavilion and periodically pulls a string which causes the figure to nod its head. Can we not imagine the delight of the younger worshippers as they bow before this image?

Now mysterious music is heard! Weird and sombre notes from horns, bells, cymbals and drums seem to issue from beneath the stage of the pavilion, and very effective it is!

The evening wears on, but we are still watching the fascinating scene. Towards midnight the thousands of pilgrims dwindle to hundreds, and we press nearer the images to have a last look. By now we can discern that they really *are* made of butter, for the heat of the lamps, plus the general warmth diffused from the crowds of pilgrims, begins to melt the figures and mar their beauty.

Many lamas armed with spades, shovels and buckets now come forward, and the butter idols are hewn to pieces and carried away. The cleanest of the material is stored away in the unused recesses of the lamasery to be kept for the base of next year's images, while the more soiled will serve for lighting purposes during the coming months.

And so ends the great Butter-God Festival! Weary in body and mind, we retire to rest with mingled feelings of pity, sorrow and longing. We have heard of heathen bowing down to gods of wood, stone, gold, silver and brass—but of *butter*? For this evening we have watched with our own eyes masses of people of many nations muttering meaningless prayers and prostrating themselves before thirty lifeless greasy images which by this time are hacked to pieces and lying in shapeless, ignominious heaps.

What does it all mean? Is it not another proof that the god of this world has blinded the minds of the Tibetans, debasing their religious instincts? Yet surely like the Athenians centuries ago, they are groping after the "Unknown God," "if haply they might feel after Him and find Him."

Such is our assurance as we visit these festivals year after year, setting up our Gospel banners, preaching deliverance from sin through the blood of Jesus Christ, and selling or distributing Scripture portions, pictures and tracts. These go out in Chinese, Arabic, Mongolian and Tibetan, and who knows how far the seed may be scattered—even to

the distant places of Mongolia, or to the remotest
lamaseries and tent encampments in the regions
beyond of Tibet?

"It shall not return unto me void, but it shall
accomplish that which I please"—our faith lays
hold of this promise as we labour year after year
at the Kumbum festivals.

CHAPTER VIII

A VISIT TO THE KOKO-NOR

SOME seventy miles west of Sining city lies the famous Koko-nor, which being interpreted means the Blue Lake. To the Tibetans, it is known by the name of Tso-anuam-bor, while the Chinese call it Tsing Hai. The name Koko-nor is supposed to have been given by the Mongols. The lake is recognized as sacred and is constantly worshipped by Tibetans from far and near. Chinese and Mongols also reverence it, and Sining officials make a yearly pilgrimage to its shores for worship.

A trip to the lake will be in great contrast to our visit to the Kumbum festivals, and not so exhausting to body and mind.

Travelling by swift horse, it would be possible to make the journey to the lakeside in two stages, but we shall find it more interesting and less strenuous to take four days to reach its shores. We must make preparations for the journey so that we may be independent, for we do not know how we shall be received as we travel. We shall hope to fall in with hospitable people who will supply us with all requisites, but on the other hand, we may meet

[*Photo by F. Doggett Learner*

THE PRAYER HALL AT THE Rï-ku-long-sï LAMASERY

[*Facing page* 112

[*Photo by F. Doggett Learner*

A CANTILEVER BRIDGE NEAR SINING

Note the ice beginning to form in the water.

with hostility and be refused both food and shelter. As a whole, however, I have proved the Tibetans a kindly and hospitable people.

Let us now get our baggage ready! A good supply of stores is advisable, and plenty of bedding, for we are going to colder climes. We shall also take a quantity of gospels and other literature, as well as many sundries. These are neatly packed away in saddlebags, each one of a pair the same weight, that they may balance across the saddle. If baggage is not rightly adjusted, it may prove an endless source of trouble on the road.

The horses are now saddled and in readiness, and after a hasty breakfast at dawn we are off, reaching the city gates as they are being thrown open. Our road lies in a westerly direction, and as we leave the city we cross over the South River by a picturesque bridge. Some thirty miles away on the distant horizon, we see the hazy outline of the La-chi mountains from which the river takes its source. Soon we enter a cultivated valley of no mean size. Undulating fields containing such crops as wheat, barley, oats, peas, beans and millet are spread out before us, making a peculiarly beautiful scene. We continue the undeviating course of this road some twenty miles up the valley, when another river stretches before us. Fortunately we can cross it by a well-constructed cantilever bridge, and we give thanks. At other points of our journey, we may have to ford rivers on horseback—a difficult task, for our animals may sometimes sink in soft mud up to their knees.

H

Now we halt for a rest at a place called Tsa-ma-leng, where there is an inn. Our horses' girths are unloosed, and after giving them time to cool off, the inn stable-boy prepares a bran mash for the animals' midday meal while we make our way to the warm *kang* within.

Friends in the home countries will be familiar with the word *kang*, and will know that in north and central China it does duty for table, chairs and bed. It is built close to the wall and varies in length according to the size of the room. It is usually constructed of bricks, the inside being left hollow for heating purposes. Dried stable refuse being ever at hand and cheaper than wood is used as fuel. The ideal *kang* has the hole for lighting and stoking in the outer wall of the house, but unfortunately it is most often within the room, and the escaping smoke is a great trial in our travels as it causes stinging throat and inflamed eyes.

Kangs in our district, however, are slightly different, for instead of the top being bricked in, narrow wooden planks are used. When a guest arrives at an inn, these planks are speedily removed and fuel is put in and lighted, whereupon they are replaced, and the *kang* is ready for occupation. Unfortunately the boards are very uneven, and seldom fit well together. The result is not conducive to sleep, for in addition to the irregularity of the planks pressing on one's body, the boards wobble in a seesaw-like manner as one changes one's position. The greatest discomfort, however, is caused by the smoke which escapes through the chinks, the odoriferous fumes from the fuel being especially trying. How often has one suffered a raging headache in consequence!

Another frequently trying experience results from the multiplicity of unseen occupants who hungrily await us on the *kang*—the unwelcome company known in Mission circles as "China's millions." Endless stories might be related of this discomfort and of the methods used to avoid being nibbled at while staying at inns. On one occasion I was compelled to seek refuge in an open manger in the inn yard, but I had not been long asleep when I was rudely awakened by a mule munching at my top hair. I "shooed" him off in double-quick time and fell into sleep again, but he returned at intervals until morning light for the same escapade. I have been asked if there is any connection between that incident and my growing baldness!

There are frequent accidents through the over-heating of the *kang*, as we know by experience in our Sining dispensary. Through carelessness of parents, children have often fallen into the fire and have been brought to us with terrible burns. Bedding is often scorched by the fire becoming too fierce, and one may feel like a roasted chestnut on one side, while the other may be shivering.

One bitterly cold evening, a fellow-missionary arrived at an inn after a long stage of travelling. The inn-keeper, anxious to heat the *kang* well, put in an extra supply of fuel for the guest's greater comfort. About midnight, the traveller awoke with a sharp pain in his leg. Moving it quickly, he caused a draught under the blankets which immediately burst into flames! But when a *kang* is satisfactorily heated and the smoke properly controlled, it is the greatest boon and cheer, especially when the mercury falls below zero.

After this digression on the comforts and discomforts of a Chinese *kang*, let us proceed on our journey! We now enter a narrow gorge of exquisite beauty following close beside the sparkling tumbling waters of the West River. We sniff exhilarating, pine-scented air, wondering whether we have been suddenly transported to Scotland. Around us are birch trees, willows, and pines dotted among the precipitous rocks and rugged boulders of the gorge. So beautiful is it that we almost forget the appalling unevenness of the track on which we journey. Fortunately we are on horseback and not in a cart, or we should not be appreciating the beauty around us so much. A Chinese cart is devoid of springs. Its framework is heavy and clumsy, and its axle is made of wood. No wonder its luckless riders suffer from aching bodies and jagged nerves, while sometimes bruises and cuts are the reward of a long day's journey.

Of special interest is an ancient wall through which we pass. It is a section of the ethnographical border wall which originally divided China from Tibet. It winds its way through valley, over hill and across plain for many tens of miles until it joins the Great Wall in the north. A fascinating expedition awaits the enthusiast who would explore its course.

By mid-afternoon, as we come over the brow of a hill, we sight the city of Tangar about two miles distant. This is the end of our first stage, and here we stay for the night. The Christians of the small church in this place give us a large-hearted welcome, treating us with lavish hospitality and doing all they possibly can for our comfort. Our fellowship with them is a mutual joy.

After a sound sleep till dawn and a simple breakfast, we continue our travels. The road being less uneven, we now proceed at a quicker pace. All is indescribably beautiful in the morning air. Now we are on the outskirts of a teak or ash forest, now by a sparkling clear stream, anon through belts of flower-studded grasslands which prove a great attraction to botanists both from America and England.

We encounter various types of people as we travel. Chinese merchants from Tibet are at first sight difficult to distinguish from Tibetans, clad as they are in sheepskin gowns. Mohammedans, too, pass us on our way. They likewise are dressed in sheepskins, with the addition of fox-fur hats, but they appear more formidable as they carry guns and have swords stuck in their belts.

Now we meet a procession of lamas on smart little horses with gaily-coloured trappings. In the centre of the file rides an Incarnate Buddha mounted on a fine steed. He is arrayed in a bright yellow satin gown lined with fox fur and bordered with tiger skin. Complete with a gold-plated helmet on his holy head, he makes a splendid picture.

Next we spy a company of Tibetans with their multitude of yak. The animals are laden with sheep's wool which will be bartered at Tangar for such merchandise as grain and flour. As they near us, intermingled with the gruntings of the yak, we hear the murmur of their voices, for in travelling they continuously and almost unconsciously repeat the mystic formula "Om mani padme hum." They cannot refrain from it—it seems to be part of their being. In passing us, however, their mutterings are interrupted, for we hear the word "Oruss!" (Russian) from many lips as we go by. Russians being the nearest "white" neighbours to Tibet, the common folk designate all westerners without distinction by that term.

A long caravan of camels now appears on the distant plain, owned by Mongols who always travel on camel back. As they approach, we notice that they are heavily laden with camping equipment, tents forming the main bulk of their baggage, though pots and pans and other paraphernalia are also much in evidence. The effect of the advancing caravan is very picturesque, for the Mongols are mostly dressed in yellow and red clothing, while camels in motion have a peculiar fascination of their own.

By midday we are feeling hungry, and our limbs are stiff from being long in the saddle, so we decide to rest awhile. Halting beside a clear sparkling stream, we proceed to unload the animals, and after hobbling them, allow them to graze at random on the luxuriance around. The process of hobbling our horses is simple. We join the forelegs loosely together with a rope and then tie it to the back right leg, allowing plenty of tether for the animal's freedom. If we omit to restrict our horses' movements, we might have difficulty in tracing them after our siesta, as they would wander far away.

We now collect *argol* (dried cattle manure) to make a fire. Selecting three large stones, we place on them our copper cauldron filled with water. The fuel is damp, so we produce our bellows from one of the saddle-bags. At first sight you will not recognize the article under that name. It consists of the whole skin of a sheep sewn tightly up except for one small opening in which is inserted a thin iron pipe about a foot in length. When manipulated by one who is skilled in the art, these ingenious bellows prove most efficient.

Having recently come from Tangar market, we have bread and meat and vegetables with us, and before long our cauldron emits a fragrant appetizing odour. In gipsy fashion we partake of the savoury stew, completing our meal with a cup of tea.

Meanwhile a party of Tibetans approaches. With Chinese ceremony, I offer one of the men a piece of bread, expecting a polite refusal—forgetting for the moment that he is a Tibetan. Eagerly he holds out his hand! Probably he has not seen white bread for long, and he is by no means desirous of refusing such a luxury!

For another hour we rest, stretching ourselves full length on the grassy carpet beneath us, and looking up to the blue vault of heaven above. Then refreshed in body and mind, we re-pack our saddle-bags, release our horses and continue our journey.

Until dusk we travel through gorgeous scenery, at intervals crossing and re-crossing a tumbling stream. Fortunately there has been no rain lately, or the stream might have become a roaring, unfordable torrent. Sometimes travellers have risked crossing when the river is rising, and have been rewarded with a good wallowing in the seething waters, while they have regretfully watched their belongings being carried away down the turbulent current.

We end our second day's journey at a village which contains a single inn. With the warm hospitality of border folk, and in contrast to the average innkeeper along the main roads of China, Mr. and Mrs. Wang do their utmost to give us comfort and rest. Sitting on the heated *kang* in friendly fashion with our host and hostess, we forget our weariness over a cup of tea, while on the other side of the wall we hear the horses lazily munching their hay and crunching their peas. They too have forgotten the trials and fatigue of the road.

Noticing a cow in the yard outside, we venture to ask Mrs. Wang if she will sell us some milk for our supper. She readily consents and goes to fetch the milking bowl. To our bewilderment and consternation, she returns to the yard carrying, in addition to the bowl, what appears to be a stuffed calf! She explains that the cow's offspring died soon after it was born, whereat in her sorrow she refused to give milk. The dilemma was overcome by the ingenious idea of cleansing the carcase and filling it with straw. As soon as the calf was put directly under the cow's nose, she sniffed and licked it contentedly and immediately acceded to our request for milk.

In the morning, after settling our account and leaving a present of some gospels and tracts, we say good-bye to our host and hostess and start on the third stage of our journey. Before midday we arrive at the lamasery of Tong-ko, where we know that we will receive a welcome, as we have been this way before. We are met at the entrance by a number of lamas who take our animals from us and lead them to the stables, while we are shown the guest-room. A huge bundle of brushwood is quickly brought, placed in the fire-pan and set alight. What matter if the smoke makes our eyes smart? Boiled tea is prepared, highly buttered, milked and salted as usual, while the barley-flour crock is not wanting. Drinking bowl after bowl of the tea concoction, and mixing our own *tsamba* with our fingers in the same bowls, we sit among our lama friends speaking of things concerning the Kingdom of God. They willingly listen to the Story of stories and accept some literature, for westerners seldom pass that way, and they are eager for all the knowledge that they can acquire. A couple of hours quickly go by, and then, refreshed by the warmth both of the tea and the welcome, and promising to return, we are escorted to the outer gate of the lamasery and start again on our travels.

Hills and tablelands are now before us, and soon we begin ascending. The exhilarating air invigorates us, and the blood tingles in our veins. How good it is to be alive! After some hours of gradual ascent, we reach the summit of the "Sun and Moon Mountain," from which the Koko-nor

suddenly breaks upon our view. We stand enraptured
by the loveliness of the scene before us—the lake
lying like a sapphire surrounded by the emerald
green of the hills. And yet how few people ever
see this wondrous beauty, for not many nomads
frequent this way and only an occasional traveller!

We are now at the boundary line between China
and Tibet, though there is nothing to mark it. Having
my camera with me, as always, we will take a photograph to celebrate the occasion, though the borders
consist only of prairie land with the Blue Lake in
the background. To my delight I see a horseman
appearing in the distance. He is a nomad and is
galloping towards us. I produce my tripod and set
up my camera in readiness. On he comes and I
wait expectantly—bulb in hand. Just as he is getting
near enough for a shot, he suddenly spies me, whereupon he speedily turns his horse's head and bolts
as if for his life! Whether he was afraid of my person
or whether he thought that the tripod was some
implement of war, we do not know. But all we see
for our picture is retreating horses' heels at full gallop,
and we refrain from exposing the film.

With our backs now on China, we gradually
descend the slope of the Sun and Moon Mountain.
All we see before us is the stretch of deep blue water
surrounded by endless grass-land. Soon we come to
level ground, though we do not forget that we are
still at a great elevation. The grass is fine and soft,
and we give our horses free rein as we gallop mile
after mile over the springy turf. Sometimes we prefer
a canter, at others an easy amble in order to rest

our horses. Flocks of cattle are browsing on the long soft grass. Herds of countless wild asses are ahead of us, but they are timid creatures, and as we approach they snort in defiance and set off at full gallop, shooting their tails straight out. Could we get a close view of one of them, we should see that the wild ass resembles a mule. Its general colour is reddish brown, though it is white at the throat and under the body. It has a short black mane, and a black line extends the whole length of its back, with a cross line running down its shoulders, giving a zebra-like effect. It resembles a zebra also in its running, which is swift and graceful. The Tibetans sometimes use the wild ass for food. Cooked with wild onions, it makes a very palatable dish.

We continue skimming over the grass-land, sometimes at an easy trot, and sometimes putting our horses to their mettle, when we seem to be almost flying in mid air. We have left the land of houses far behind us, and are now passing tent-dwelling nomads in their encampments. As we have opportunity, we visit the tents and distribute literature.

After some hours' further travelling, we come to the "Temple of the Lake god" where we are able to stay for the night. We are now about fifty *li* from the Koko-nor though it seems but a stone's throw, lit up as it is with the splendour of a flaming sunset. Of recent years the Temple of the Lake god has been much neglected, and no lamas are in residence. It is only inhabited at special times, one of which is the yearly pilgrimage of the Sining officials with their retinue. We therefore find it in an untidy condition, but it will serve well for a night's shelter, as we need protection from the cold biting winds that sweep over the high tableland. As we are prepared with plenty of food and bedding, we pass the night in comparative comfort, and next morning, after a few hours' final gallop, we arrive at our goal—the shores of the Koko-nor!

What an expanse of blueness! How clear and cold the water as we bathe our faces and hands in it! A hardy enthusiast may dare to take a plunge, but even in summer the water stings like a lash. The keenness of the air acts as an invigorating tonic, while the stillness and peace of the scene before us enter our souls. Here in the solitude we are "far from the madding crowd" of a Chinese city, where we are always at the beck and call of many —and we pray that the memories of the calm and tranquillity around may remain with us in the coming years.

We would like to travel around the lake, but it is 230 miles in circumference, and we cannot spare the twenty days which the journey would take. Neither have we the necessary Tibetan guide, for there would be the seventy-two rivers which feed its waters to ford. So we camp out where we are, recalling as we rest some geographical facts about the lake. There is a legend, too, which I once heard concerning the origin of this great inland salt sea. Centuries ago, it is said, there was a mysterious subterranean passage extending from Lhassa to the place where the lake now is. Through that mystic tunnel Lhassa poured its sacred waters until the lake was formed, when the flow miraculously ceased. Hence the sacredness of the Koko-nor!

Having no outlet, its waters are salt and abound with fish. During the season, fish are transported in a frozen state to the Sining market. Large quantities of salt are also taken to Sining, but although this salt is supposed to have been procured from the Koko-nor, in reality it is obtained from a dry lake to the south-west. The surface salt of this lake-bed is of snowy whiteness, but as it has lost much of its savour, the Tibetans dig down for the pure crystal salt which is found beneath. This is sent across China to far-off places.

It will be remembered that there are five islands on the lake. The four smaller ones are uninhabited as the land is rocky and uncultivable. The fifth is larger and possesses a cave lamasery where a number of lamas live. They are the only inhabitants of the island. They cultivate their own crops beside owning cattle and sheep, and thus are independent of the outside world. This is fortunate, as the island is about thirty miles from the nearest shores, and owing to treacherous squalls and violent winds which sometimes arise, small boats are unsafe on the waters of the lake.

During three months of the winter, however, when the lake is frozen over, the island is no longer cut off from the mainland, and there is opportunity for pilgrims to visit the lamasery. One special pilgrimage is held during this time when large numbers of people go over the ice on foot. The lamas look forward to their coming, as they have had no news of the outside world for many months. They appreciate, too, the many presents of food which the pilgrims bring them, especially such luxuries as sugar and spices. The journey of thirty miles on ice is a long day's travelling for the pilgrims, and they always go in companies, as blizzards and storms may suddenly arise.

Some years ago, three European explorers desired to visit the island. It was summer time, so they devised a collapsible canvas boat just big enough to hold them. Waiting for a favourable wind, and hoisting an improvised sail, they soon covered the distance and made a safe landing. No one was to be seen, but a trodden path led from the shore, and they followed it to a cave which showed signs of habitation. Not a soul was in sight within the cave, but hearing the murmur of voices in the distance, they groped their way along darkened passages until they came to a room cut out of the rocks. A small aperture in the wall let in enough light for them to see some lamas sitting on a low bench. Their backs were turned to the visitors. The room was evidently the sanctum, and the lamas were engaged in their daily devotions. They continued their incantations, and the visitors were wondering whether they should silently withdraw when one of the lamas suddenly turned his head. As he saw the strangers, he experienced a terrible fright! The explorers with signs and gesticulations tried to explain the circumstances, but it was not until the lamas had gone down to the shore and the canvas boat had been inspected that they became calm. Never had such a thing been heard of before, and the holy men had thought the travellers must be an apparition of demons from the nether world! Neither had they ever seen a westerner, which fact naturally increased their astonishment. When the situation was understood, the lamas proved themselves friendly and hospitable, inviting their guests to stay the night in the lamasery. In the morning the visitors set sail across the lake, the lamas watching from the shore till the skiff was out of sight.

The goal of our travelling is attained! We have spent some hours at the lake-side, and now we must retrace our steps to Sining. As on our outward journey, so on our homeward we will distribute literature as we have opportunity, praying that it may be kept and read long after our spoken messages are forgotten. For this great work of the distribution of Christian books, we are bountifully supplied by the Scripture Gift Mission, and the Tibetan Religious Literature Depot, as well as by the Bible Societies.

In recent times the people have been far more ready to accept gospels and tracts than they were in the past. During my visit to this region very many years ago, I remember seeing an old Tibetan caring for his flock of sheep beside the lake. In my youthful enthusiasm, I approached him offering one of my books. I shall never forget the look of fear on the old man's face! Whether it was that he was startled at being offered something for nothing, or scared at the sudden apparition of a barbarian, I do not know —probably both. But I made myself as friendly as I could, and after some persuasion he accepted my leaflet.

And so God's servants leave behind these silent messengers wherever they go, and portions of Scripture are scattered all over Tibet. Our effort is a feeble one, but we dare not fail to present the Word of Life both through literature and by spoken messages.

When Moses, feeling his incompetence for the task God had given him, began to make excuses, did not God ask him, "What is that in thine hand?" And did not our Master say to the lad with the loaves and fishes, "Bring them hither to me"?

God used Moses' rod and the boy's food for His own glory, and will He not also use the gospels and tracts which we carry in our hands? In faith we believe that He does.

CHAPTER IX

AMONG THE NOMADS

On our trip to the Koko-nor Lake, we had not sufficient time to visit the nomads' tents at leisure, so we will plan another itinerary that we may accomplish this and have further opportunities of distributing literature. Tibetan nomads live exclusively in tents, and there are even some lamaseries in the far interior which are comprised entirely of tents. Usually, however, as the reader already knows, lamaseries consist of a series of solid and highly decorative buildings.

For our coming itineration we must again make careful preparations, and in addition to a quantity of literature, bedding, cooking utensils and food, we will equip ourselves with a number of small articles to serve as presents to the tent-dwellers, not forgetting a goodly supply of *khata* which we never omit to carry with us. The presents which are always acceptable to the nomads are such things as scissors, knives, mirrors, beads, needles and tapes.

As we are going across mountain passes to higher altitudes, our own city horses will not be able for the hardships of the way, and we shall ride Tibetan horses. These are much smaller, but they are sturdy and tough and are accustomed to the severe cold and the coarser grass food of their own climes.

The alternative to the Tibetan horse is the yak, but we unanimously decide not to risk our persons to their untender mercies. The yak possesses a fiery and fickle temper, and as its rider can guide it only by tugging at a rope attached to a ring through its nose, it is almost impossible to control. When there are a number of yak, they always persist in travelling huddled together, clumsily barging and bumping into each other, so that their riders' legs are often battered and bruised at the end of a day. Their unhappy habit, too, of suddenly rushing up a steep bank or of rolling in a river is somewhat trying, while if the beast feels its burden becoming too heavy, it may decide on a sudden somersault as the most efficient line of action. Moreover, it seems to be always on the look-out for food as it travels, and should it be near a precipice, the grass on the extreme edge will assuredly be considered sweeter and more appetizing than that beside the path. The continual grunting of the yak is also extremely wearing to the westerner, so for these and other reasons the missionary spares himself the nerve-trying experience of travelling on yak back, and prefers the trusty little Tibetan horse for his journeys. On such a trip as this it is essential to take with me Tong-fuh-tang, the Tibetan evangelist (of whom more later), as my knowledge of the Tibetan language is so limited.

Let us now suppose that we are cantering over the velvety grass-clad tablelands far beyond the border. Suddenly some Tibetan tents appear to view! I

ITINERATING IN TIBET

Above : On the Road.

Below : Crossing a mountain pass 15,000 feet high on the Tibetan
Border.

[*Photos by F. Doggett Learner*

CAMELS AND YAK ON THE TIBETAN BORDER
Above : A string of camels travelling towards Tibet.
Below : Yak laden with sheep's wool from Tibet for the Sining market.

say "suddenly", because a place of encampment is always chosen in some hollow or behind a hillock, so that the tents may be partially sheltered from the biting winds which sweep across these vast prairie lands. One seldom sees a solitary tent. They are to be found in groups of six or seven.

A Tibetan tent reminds one of a huge black spider! Within are two perpendicular poles and one horizontal—the mainstays of the tent. Without are a great number of staves and ropes tethering it securely to the ground so that in times of hurricane it may be safe. The heavy black cloth of which it is constructed is made from yak hair by hand loom and is exceedingly strong. A trench is dug around the tent in order to drain away the water during the rainy season.

Every Tibetan tent-dweller owns watch-dogs—huge fierce creatures that will not hesitate to take life if an enemy trespasses. Around each tent is a border line, sometimes only imaginary, within which the dogs are taught to watch. If we desire to visit the tent-dwellers, we must first direct their attention to our approach, and the ferocious brutes will be warded off.

The memories of an experience of many years ago will always remain with me. A fellow-missionary, Mr. Mark Botham, and I were visiting the nomads' tents with literature. Approaching unawares within the borders of an almost hidden encampment, we were suddenly surrounded by a pack of these fierce dogs. What followed proved to be a race for our lives! The bloodthirsty beasts kept up alongside of our horses for a mile or so, hoping to drag us from the saddle. One angry monster made a mark of my right foot in the stirrup, and it was with the greatest difficulty that I was able to keep it out of his reach. It is no easy matter to maintain one's balance in the saddle when galloping one's hardest with one foot raised high. The situation was precarious. Were our lives in a few minutes' time to be ignominiously ended on these Tibetan prairies?

Now fortunately a short time previously we had picked up a dry bone on the shores of the Koko-nor, intending to keep it as a souvenir of our first trip to the Lake. Just when all seemed up with us, for our horses were flagging, we remembered this bone. My friend had it in his pocket, and flung it his hardest to the beast which was nearest him. The dog stopped short and went in search of it. Like a pack of ravenous wolves, the other brutes were speedily on his track. Now was our opportunity! We continued galloping as best we could for a while longer, but on turning round and seeing no trace of the dogs, we brought our horses to a standstill and flung ourselves on to the grass. We were safe! Both man and beast were panting for breath and we rested there some time before continuing our journey. Sometimes when I linger on past reminiscences, I recall the occasion when our lives were saved by a bone, and although it is not in our possession, the memory is still a souvenir of thankfulness to God's protective care.

In later years I learned the right method of approach to a Tibetan tent. While still well outside the border line, I attract the attention of its inmates by hallooing,

or if they already see me, by shouting that I wish to
call on them. After ascertaining that I am not an
undesirable visitor, the head of the family comes
out to greet me and to ward off the dogs. A Tibetan
places implicit trust in his dogs though they are almost
untamable. If necessary he would use his gun or his
sword to repel an attack on himself or others. Usually,
however, at the sight of them, the dogs are cowed.

While still at a distance, the owner of the tent
asks who I am and what my business is. I reply
that I am an Englishman from the Tibetan Gospel
Inn in Sining. That is sufficient credential, for our
Gospel Inn has already earned a good name throughout the district. Meanwhile I am observing the staid
demeanour and quiet gravity of the man before
me, and I am admiring his stalwart, muscular
physique, his arms and chest bronzed by exposure
to all weathers. When I have won his approval, he
advances towards me, and with Tibetan ceremony
I produce my *khata* in salutation. Holding it with
both hands, I place it on his outstretched arms. Now
he brings forth the return scarf from the bulky folds
of his breast pocket and ceremoniously presents it
to me. After this preliminary exchange of civilities,
our host suddenly shoots out his tongue which reaches
to the tip of his chin, simultaneously putting up his
two thumbs, and I politely do likewise, being glad
no one is near with a camera! "Arow, de-mo-ing",
he says—the Tibetan equivalent of "Friend, how do
you do?", and I make a suitable reply.

The horses are now unsaddled, the packs being
taken inside the tent, and the animals hobbled that

they may not stray too far. I am invited into the tent, and I must stoop well down as the entrance is low. The sides are low too, but in the centre one can stand upright. In the middle of the tent there is a huge fire in an open grate, and I am asked to sit down on some sheepskins before it. Over the fire hangs a big cauldron of boiling tea. Although there is a small aperture in the canvas above, by no means all of the smoke escapes through it, and the fuel used being the same as at Chinese inns, the fumes are extremely trying to one's eyes.

Now is the opportunity for me to offer a little present, and the small pair of scissors which I produce from my pocket is graciously accepted, and will be prized for many years to come.

Meanwhile I am glancing round the tent. Its furniture is simple, for there is neither chair, table nor bench to be seen. The few possessions are kept on the floor. All around the edges of the canvas there are bales of wool and sacks of grain to keep out the wind. They remind me of the "sandbags" put on the floor at the foot of draughty doors in the old farm home of my childhood. Piles of sheep-skins and bundles of clothes are to be seen too. My attention is especially drawn, however, to the top end of the tent where there is placed a little shrine containing an idol. Butter lamps and incense are burning, and at intervals through the day many prostrations are made before it.

Now my host is calling attention to the cauldron of tea and asks for my bowl, for in Tibet everyone carries his own with him. The bowls are made of the wood of a certain shrub. Wealthy Tibetans often have them lined with silver. I pass my bowl as requested, but on examining it, my polite host thinks it looks a little dusty, whereat he licks it clean with his long tongue before filling it from the cauldron. By the consistency and odour of the tea, I know that it has been boiling for a long time, and as he pours it into my bowl, it looks extremely like pea soup. He now calls his wife to bring out the oldest butter—for has not the guest come all the way from England to visit this humble tent? The woman goes to a dark recess in a corner, and as she uncovers it, the aroma that fills the tent assures me that the butter has been kept for many years. Its rancidity is apt to take the edge off my appetite, and I watch with dismay as a small chunk of the odorous delicacy is floated on the surface of my tea. I politely take the bowl from my host's hands and put it to my lips. The flavour of the age-long butter proves noxious, but I drink the beverage with a smiling countenance. Neither am I allowed to see the bottom of my bowl, for as we sit round the cauldron sipping tea and chatting in friendly intercourse, the tea bowls are filled time and again. After a while, from sheer incapacity, I have to beg to be excused from taking more. Fortunately it is not considered impolite! On the other hand, it causes amusement that I can drink so little.

Now is the time for making *tsamba* and the baked barley flour is brought out. As we have been drinking the soupy tea, we have blown aside the

floating butter, so that by the time we have disposed
of several bowls of tea, there is a quantity of butter
left. My host now fills my bowl half full of tea,
and then on top of it lodges a handful or two of
the baked barley flour. The making of *tsamba* is
quite an art. First one finger is inserted, and the
contents of the bowl gently stirred. A second finger
follows, stirring as before. A third is added, and
finally the whole hand is used in kneading the
mixture into a stiff paste. Now it is taken out of
the bowl—which should be left quite clean—and
kneaded until it becomes an even dough, when it
is ready for eating. I well remember the merriment
I caused when first I tried to make *tsamba*—spilling
a quantity of the flour around on the floor, and
leaving my bowl in a horrible mess.

Our empty bowls are now refilled with tea, and
with the newly-made *tsamba* in one hand and the
bowl in the other, we continue our afternoon tea.
Fortunately the *tsamba* is not unpleasant when the
butter is not too rancid. Like many other things
one becomes accustomed to it, but I always try to
forget that my hands were not washed before the
making, and I am most thankful that it is Tibetan
ceremony to make one's own *tsamba*.

By now the sun is setting and the family returns
to the tent after watching their cattle and sheep
on the grass-land. The duty of milking the yak
cows falls to the young women, and this is no small
task, for I see between twenty and thirty yak being
tethered in readiness. The man and his wife are
busy preparing the evening meal, so I take a stroll

outside. It is dusk and the stars are beginning to twinkle in the darkening sky. As I watch the milk-maids busy at their work, I recall with amusement a similar occasion many years ago when for the first time I saw yak being milked.

Having an electric torch in my hand, I unthinkingly flashed it towards the scene that I might see better. Now yak are timid creatures, and not being used to so brilliant a light, they were so startled that they all broke loose in panic, pulling up the pegs in the ground by which they were tethered, and galloping off to the four winds, grunting and snorting their unanimous disapproval. To make matters worse, the full pails of milk were upset in the stampede. I shall not readily forget the volleys of cursing and swearing that issued forth from the lips of the grand-mother of the tent. When after an hour or two the disgruntled cows were again caught and tethered, nothing would persuade them to yield more milk, and they kept up their gruntings all through the night.

I am recalled from my reverie by the appetizing fragrance which is wafted on the cold evening air from within the tent, and my host is calling me to supper. I re-enter the tent, which is now lit by several small butter lamps, and soon every one is sitting on the sheepskins around a giant cauldron over the re-kindled fire.

When all is ready, the lid is removed and I am invited to help myself from its contents. With the aid of my knife, I succeed in capturing a chunk of mutton, or it may be yak meat. I drop it into my bowl to allow it to cool and then I eat it with

relish.   The members of the family are not shy of
their English guest, and having been in the open
air all day, have come to the evening meal with
healthy appetites.   Drawing their knives from the
sheaths which always hang from their belts, the
men and women hack off hunk after hunk of the
meat from the seething cauldron.   How they manage
to hold the boiling meat in their hands I do not
know!   They eat ravenously and with extraordinary
speed until I marvel at their internal capacity.

Meanwhile with the fierce heat of the fire, and
with the added warmth caused by devouring hot
food, the countenances of the tent-dwellers are
glistening with liquid butter.   As it melts, it trickles
slowly down face and arms and chest, and the
atmosphere becomes somewhat odoriferous.   By this
time the meat in the pot has diminished.   Tea-
bowls are now produced from the breast pocket
hold-all, and dipping them in the cauldron, we
proceed to scoop out the gravy.   How delicious it
is!   After filling and emptying them many times,
bowls are licked clean and returned to the pocket.
The meal is now complete.

We continue sitting round the fire talking of many
things.   They are eager to hear all I can relate
about my country, and in their turn they tell me
many things concerning their own people with their
customs and beliefs.   I like to watch their interesting
faces, and I wish I could produce a moving picture
of the scene before me.   The dying fire lights up
the eager though buttery features of the men and
women, the boys and the girls.   The women, though

quieter than the men, are not so shy as they were
when I first arrived.

Now is the opportunity for the message which I
have come to deliver, and I tell them (through Tong-
fuh-tang) the Old, Old Story. They have never
heard of Jesus before and they listen with eyes aglow,
asking questions from time to time. My heart is full
of joy as I realize afresh the privilege that is ours
in being heralds of the Glad Tidings we have come
to bring.

By now it is time to settle in for the night. The
transformation of the tent from a dining-room to
a bedroom is simple. The cauldron is removed,
more fuel is put on the fire, and, spreading out the
sheepskins, the family prepares for sleep. Undoing
my bundle of bedding, I stretch my weary body
upon it and cover myself with my blankets. Nights
in this altitude, however, being much colder than
at Sining, I am glad of a few extra sheepskins on
the top of my rugs.

Picture the interior of the tent! The whole family
is lying around covered with sheepskins, while little
calves or goats or lambs have been brought in to
share the comfort and warmth of the tent in case
they should perish in the cold outside. One of them
is nestling down beside me. The yak and horses—
my own among them—are tethered just outside
the tent, and the trusty watch-dogs are guarding
the entrance. As I lie surrounded by the Tibetan
family, I can see their forms by the glowing light
of the fire, and I know by their heavy breathing
and snoring that they are soundly asleep. Outside,

the night is dark and eerie. I hear the grunting of the yak and the occasional screech of an owl. At intervals the weird howl of wolves is heard. They are prowling around seeking for food to satisfy their hunger—and I snuggle down under my blankets.

But for me, sleep seems far away. Now my mind is recounting the experiences of the day, now it is considering to-morrow's itineration, now it is yearning for a laddie in Chefoo, now thinking of a lonely wife and small daughter in Sining, and now it is spanning the seas and is with dear ones in the homeland for whom it is still early afternoon. What are they doing just now? How amused they would be to see me in such surroundings! And O, in this atmosphere, for the scent of the home roses!

My ruminations dissolve into prayer, returning as so often to the comforting thought of the "common mercy seat" . . . and after committing myself and my all to His changeless, ever-watchful care, oblivious now to my environment, my weary body and mind sink into peaceful slumber.

CHAPTER X

THE DOOR IS OPENING

HAVE you ever had the experience of opening an old barn door which has been kept shut for some years? The creaking and jarring of its rusty hinges, as with an effort it is forced open, may be used as a simile of the long-closed doors of Tibet. In bygone decades, this vast land has been closed to the Gospel, but now its doors are grating on their time-worn hinges, and a transformation is coming over the people. It is true that they are still bound as if with shackles, but these are gradually being loosed. During recent years a change towards the missionary and his message is markedly perceptible, and the time will come, we pray in faith, when Tibetans will be liberated from the fetters which bind them.

My own small share in this work has been in response to a call which came to me in the year 1920. I had then lived in Sining for seven years and great opporunties for evangelistic work among the Chinese had been mine. But I had all the time noticed Tibetans coming and going between Sining and their own land, and beyond occasional gifts of Christian literature, nothing definite was being done to bring the Gospel to them. This fact was a real burden on my mind, and I continually besought God for a clear answer to my prayers concerning it.

My call—for I can use no other word—was heard while on a visit to the Kumbum lamasery. I had taken tracts and gospels with me, but I had a very limited knowledge of the Tibetan language then, and the attempt to impart the great message to the lamas' understanding seemed very feeble.

One afternoon, feeling burdened with a sense of their need, I walked up a hill at the back of the lamasery. Sitting on the grassy slopes, I gazed at the mountains which separate China from Tibet. Their peaks were sparkling in the afternoon sun, and as my eyes rested on the purity of their whiteness, the question, "But what is beyond?" thrust itself upon me. I thought of the millions of lips uttering meaningless prayers, millions of bodies daily bowed in prostrations, millions of people awaiting the blessing of men who call themselves Incarnate Buddhas. And so little was being done to bring the Light to them!

Suddenly it seemed as if a voice was speaking! "I want *you* to do something for these people!"

The words were so clear in my mind that I knew it was God speaking in the silence.

"Lord, I am willing to do anything that You want me to do, but give me a sign that I may know Your will more clearly!" I asked too that the sign might be given before our approaching furlough.

The months passed and no other definite leading had been given. Soon my wife and I would have to start on our long trek to the coast. There was one place to be visited, however, as a matter concerning the Church there had to be dealt with. So the journey of several miles to the city of Mao-peh-sheng was taken. The Church business settled, on the morrow I was to return to Sining.

That evening I was sitting having my meal in the Mohammedan inn where I was staying, when a knock was heard at the door. In response to my "Enter!" in walked two men—a Tibetan unknown to me, and a Chinese Christian, an old friend, whose home was in a city fully twenty miles distant. After they were seated my friend told me that they had heard I was at Mao-peh-sheng, and that they had come to visit me as this Tibetan wished to become a Christian. At that, I nearly jumped off my seat with joy and surprise!

I at once invited them to share my evening meal and as we partook of our "mien" together (a sort of vermicelli made of wheaten flour) I learned that the Tibetan had a rudimentary knowledge of the Gospel through the Chinese Christian, Mr. Ting, who had recently told him something of the Good News. We sat and talked on till a late hour, concluding with reading of the Word and prayer together.

That day, instead of returning immediately to Sining, I accepted the invitation of the Tibetan enquirer—whose name is Chi-fah-chia—to visit his home some ten miles distant. A walk through beautiful mountain scenery brought us to the village where he lived, and I was received with open hospitality

—his wife and sons and daughters welcoming us, and a sheep being killed in preparation for the midday meal. We spent some hours in the house, impressing on him the seriousness of the step which he wanted to take, and warning him that suffering and persecution would come if he became a Christian. But he had made up his mind!

After commending him to God in prayer, I went on my way with a joyful heart. Surely this was the sign my wife and I had been praying for. Surely the one Tibetan seeking after God was our call and encouragement to start definite work among those others who came to Sining, and with this glad assurance in our hearts, we started for furlough.

In the home country we met with many friends who listened eagerly to the story of our hopes and plans, and in the fullness of time we joyfully returned with permission and funds with which to start an Inn or Hostel for Tibetans visiting Sining.

After but a short delay, we were able to purchase a property consisting of a few rooms enclosing a fair-sized courtyard adjoining our own Mission premises. A good deal of renovating and alteration, with extra buildings, was needed, but a very suitable place was the result of the planning and work.

Now came the preparation for the official opening of the premises. The date fixed had been December 1st. (It was in the year 1923). It had been advertised with placards in Tibetan and Chinese character posted up all over the city. In addition, ceremonial invitations had been sent to the civil and military officials, as well as to teachers in Government schools and to most of the influential gentry and literati of the city. The place was tastefully decorated with flags, festoons, scrolls and banners, as well as large Bible pictures and coloured sheet tracts in Tibetan character. The effect was very attractive and pleasing to the eye.

At the upper end of the courtyard a platform was erected with forms and chairs facing it. As the guests arrived, tea à la Tibetan was served with Chinese cakes. The majority of the people, among whom were a number of Tibetans, took their seats in the open courtyard, but the officials were conducted to some rooms behind the platform which had been decorated and furnished befittingly. There they reclined comfortably in foreign arm-chairs, and the doors and windows being open, they could hear well.

The proceedings commenced at one o'clock. At a given signal by the herald, all rose from their seats and made three deep bows to the Chinese flag. At that time it was the five-bar emblem of red, yellow, blue, white and black, representing China, Manchuria, Mongolia, the Moslems and Tibet. This was followed by the singing of the Chinese Christian National Anthem and another national song composed for the occasion.

Now came the chairman's opportunity for laying the needs and aims of the Gospel Inn before the big audience. His talk was based on "God . . . Who will have all men to be saved, and to come unto the knowledge of the truth." It was pointed out that the Scriptures or "Holy Classics" were now printed in over eight hundred languages or dialects, five of these being used in the Sining district, namely,

K

Chinese, Arabic, Mongol, Kalmuk and Tibetan.
A quotation from the Chinese classics, "All within
the four seas are brothers", showed that the Tibetans
are our near kindred. Sining had been opened as
a Mission station more than thirty years ago, but
nothing definite had been done to bring the Tibetans
of the district "unto the knowledge of the truth".
Now the way had been cleared, the doors opened,
and to-day these premises were to be dedicated to
the glory of God, and in His Name the Gospel was
to be preached to the Tibetans who would come to
reside in the Hostel.

Four other addresses followed. The late famous
Mohammedan General Ma-chi, although present,
did not speak himself, but his representative, in
offering the General's congratulations, discoursed
favourably on missionary endeavours. The second
official of the city, the Intendant of the Circuit,
gave a really excellent address, and although he
is not a Christian, he commended Christian truths
and beliefs to the large audience. The last two
speeches were given by members of the church, and
in them the Gospel banner was lifted high.

Now came a short interlude of music. Two
missionaries sang a duet in Tibetan, after which an
English hymn was sung by about thirty schoolboys.
Both seemed to be greatly enjoyed by the audience.

What followed was the item of central significance—
the Dedication of the Hostel. All stood reverently
with bared heads while the Dedicatory Prayer was
offered, and then the Benediction brought the ceremony
to a close.

No special occasion in China would be complete without a photograph, and a great deal of time is always spent in the grouping of it. After this had been accomplished and the picture taken, the guests were free to survey the premises at will. Many of the visitors had presented congratulatory scrolls and banners, and these were now hung in various parts of the buildings.

Let us follow our guests that we may visualize the general plan of the premises ourselves! Over the entrance we notice Tibetan characters which mean "The True Gospel Hall," though it is commonly called whether in Tibetan, English or Chinese, "The Tibetan Gospel Inn."

The compound comprises three courtyards, one leading into the other, the whole length being about forty-five yards. The lower courtyard is used for stable accommodation, for no Tibetan comes without his animal, be it horse, mule, camel, donkey or yak. This stable will hold about thirty animals, but it often proves too small. (One day a Mongolian prince arrived with a caravan of nearly a hundred camels. On that occasion we sent his animals to a camel inn in another part of the city). Around the lower courtyard are kitchens and outhouses.

Next we come to the central courtyard where we are at once attracted by the chief building of the premises—the brightly-painted Chapel. Come inside with me! Its walls are decorated with Bible pictures and large sheets of coloured texts in Tibetan. We notice that the building will seat about fifty people. On leaving the Chapel, we follow through to the upper courtyard around which are most of the guest rooms. Each room is furnished with a *kang*, a table and a fire-pan. The *kang* has space enough for five or six guests. Kettles, teapots and some crockery are also provided. The rooms are clean and compact. How we would welcome such comfort and cleanliness on our travels across China when we must often stay in filthy, dilapidated inns!

The Tibetan Gospel Inn was now open and we began to hope for guests. Well-meaning friends told us that we must be ready for disappointment, for Tibetans might be too timid and superstitious to come to us. The days passed one by one—the weeks also. It seemed possible that the prediction might be correct, but our courage and faith did not diminish and we prayed constantly for the fulfilment of our desires.

One day, more than a month after the official opening, an old lama appeared at the inn door! No adjective can adequately express our joy! The old man was sick and he had come for medicine. We took him in and cared for him until he was well —a space of two or three weeks. The ice was broken! Soon afterwards an Incarnate Buddha with his retinue requested to be put up at the Inn, and this helped to give us prestige.

From that time to this we have never lacked guests. In the summer months fewer come, for Tibetans avoid the heat of lower latitudes, but in the winter we have as many guests as we can receive. They come mostly for trading purposes, though a great many pilgrims visit Sining in order to worship at the Tibetan temple close by. This temple is famous, for it was built before the city walls and is over a thousand years old. Recently it has been renovated, and as it is decorated with all the colours of the rainbow, it is extremely attractive. It contains an enormous idol representing Buddha, which Tibetans from far and near come to worship. Our Gospel Inn therefore has a unique opportunity for work among the pilgrims.

Accommodation at the Inn is free, though visitors provide their own food. They cook in the kitchen of the lower courtyard, fuel being supplied gratis. Whereas in the past Tibetans had to go in search of rooms at Chinese inns, to be cheated at the will of the inn-keepers, now they come to convenient quarters where friends welcome them.

In our first year, we received as many as eight hundred visitors, and since then numbers have been on the increase. None go away without having heard of Jesus Christ. A short service is held every evening in the Chapel where the singing is always an attraction. Attendance is not compulsory though nearly all guests desire to be present. Those who remain in their rooms are visited by our cheerful evangelist, Tong-fuh-tang, whose story will, I think, make a fitting close to this chapter.

His father was a Manchu, while his mother was Tibetan. In appearance and manners and speech he resembles his mother's people more than the Manchu.

Some years ago a Tibetan was being treated in the leprosy department of the Borden Memorial Hospital in Lanchow. During his several months in the hospital, this man heard much of the Gospel from Dr. George King and before he left he obtained a copy of the New Testament. His leprosy yielded to the treatment given, and, free from all signs of the disease, he returned to his home.

Now Tong-fuh-tang was Postmaster in that place, and one day the aforetime leper was visiting the Post Office and offered to lend him the Testament. Being of studious bent, Tong-fuh-tang eagerly accepted it. The reading of the Testament led to the change in his life, and he came over to Sining, two days' journey away, to tell us his desire to become a Christian. We soon realized that he was sincere, and after a while he was baptized and received into the Church. So earnest was he that we asked him to become an evangelist in the Tibetan Gospel Inn. Although we could only offer him a much smaller salary than that which he received as Postmaster, he joyfully accepted the post. This surely was of the Lord's doing.

Since his appointment he has proved himself capable, enthusiastic and earnest. He is of cheerful disposition and is just as happy when sweeping the courtyard as he is while preaching the Gospel. His work is generally to look after the guests in the Inn, lead the services, and to tell of the Heavenly Father's love to all who enter.

May he long be spared for this great service!

CHAPTER XI

MY story is almost told but not ended. It is to be continued in the lives of the men and women who surrender to the call of Jesus Christ, whether in response to the work of the Tibetan Gospel Inn or as we continually pass through the open doors into the interior of the great land.

Soon after our return from furlough in 1923, we had the inexpressible joy of baptizing Chi-fah-chia, and his is the first Tibetan name on our Sining Church register. The reader will remember that it was this man seeking me in Mao-peh-sheng which seemed to be the sign to start evangelistic work among Tibetans.

Chi-fah-chia had apparently balanced things up pretty well before he came to see me that day long ago. He knew the testing and ridicule that might come, and he has suffered bitter persecution for his Lord. The lamas who own the land on which he lives have beaten him unmercifully, while his land taxes, which must be paid to the nearest lamasery, have been multiplied. On more than one occasion, he has been shut up in the lamasery prison, during which time, by order of the Incarnate Buddha, he has been chained to the ground in such a way as neither to be able to sit down nor stand up day and night. To hear him humbly and uncomplainingly tell his story brings tears to one's eyes.

His outward witness has been fearless and unhesitating. It is the custom in every Tibetan home to erect a pole in the middle of the courtyard, a long flag bearing Tibetan prayers attached to it. It is called a "mani" pole. Soon after Chi-fah-chia's conversion, this flag was replaced by a twenty-four feet long banner bearing the words, "The Kingdom of God is at hand! Repent ye and believe the Gospel!" The pole stands high up from the ground, and as the banner flutters in the wind, its message may be read by all.

Chi-fah-chia has won at least one other soul for Christ. This man, by the name of Tang-seng-fuh, was sixty-one years of age when Chi-fah-chia first began telling him of the Gospel. Two years later he was baptized in our Sining Church. We have visited his home many times, and our only regret is that his family, though not openly opposed, have not accepted Christianity. It seems that fear of the lamas has kept them from taking the step.

Once, hearing he was ill, I set out to visit him. I found the dear old man on his bed where he had lain several weeks. Owing to his long illness his eyesight had dimmed. He could no longer see to read his Bible and hymn book, but he had a treasured store in his heart. I was amazed to find how many hymns and passages of Scripture he could repeat, and they were his comfort and solace from morning to night. Before we left, he called

[Photos by F. Doggett Learner

Above: A Tibetan Encampment. (Note the monster watch dogs.)
Below: Chi-fah-chia and his Wife.

went back to his seat without further ado, and the service continued.

The next day I invited Lha-jar to my office for a talk. Fearing that he did not realize all that it involved, I told him of the oppression and persecution he might meet with. But he remained firm in his decision, and after I had commended him to God, he started joyfully on his long journey back to his tent.

We were able from time to time to obtain the news that he was true to his faith. We do not know to what extent, but he too suffered persecution from the lamas, as well as from the people around his home. We were told also of the change in his life. Formerly he had been known as a robber and even a murderer, but now he was a new creature in Christ Jesus. We give God all the glory for this dear old man's conversion, and we go on our way with buoyant courage.

Here is another instance showing that the messages spoken in our Gospel Inn are remembered. A missionary was recently travelling in an unfrequented part of the country not far from Sining. He was accompanied by a Chinese evangelist, and as they were passing near to a Tibetan village, they heard someone singing, "Jesus loves me, this I know," in Tibetan. Their curiosity was aroused, and turning their horses in the direction of the sound, they found a Tibetan singing at his work. On asking where he had learnt the hymn, he told them that he had heard it at the Tibetan Gospel Inn where he had lately been staying.

And so the seed is sown! Some of it doubtless
falls on stony or thorny ground and much by the
wayside, but our hearts are full of praise to God
that some falls on prepared ground and brings forth
fruit, even if only thirtyfold.

There is in the Tibetan heart, as in all humanity
the world over, a yearning for the true way, a groping
for peace, a hunger for righteousness. In Tibet this
may be illustrated in a very realistic manner by the
hermits who live in the caves of holy mountains.
There they exist year after year, relying on friends
or relatives to put food on a platter at the mouth of
the cave. The aperture is often so small that only
a shrivelled hand can be stretched out to receive
the food. Some of these "holy men" are built into
mud or stone enclosures within the lamasery to which
they belong. They have taken vows of silence and
have cut themselves off from all life's good things
hoping to obtain Nirvana. How are these hermits
to be told of God's love? We have the Gospel
which breaks every fetter, but how can these
men ever know of the One Who died to set them
free?

Recently we have been reading of the conquest by
air of the world's highest peak—Mount Everest.
Forethought, concentrated study, long, sustained
practice, and, above all, the supreme courage and
determination of the four heroes, are the human
factors which stand out in the great adventure. Is
not their magnificent feat a challenge to Missions?
Shall the Christian Church be less courageous in
taking the Word of Life over the perilous mountains

and rushing torrents of Tibet? Is the splendid missionary venture on a lower plane? I think not.

Have you read the words of Sadhu Sundar Singh in one of his calls to service and sacrifice?—"O young men! Awake and see how many souls are daily perishing around you! Is it not your duty to save them? Be brave soldiers of Christ! Go forward in full armour! Crush Satan's work, and victory be yours! God has given you a precious opportunity to save others. If you are careless now, you may never get another chance. Whatever you have to do, do it now, for you will never pass through the field of battle again. The day is fast approaching when you will see the martyrs in their glory who gave their health, wealth and life to win souls for Christ. They have done much! What have you done?"

A Chinese Christian once said, "China has three crises—a closed door and a closed heart: a closed door and an open heart: an open door and an open heart—and the third is the crisis to-day!" Surely "an open door and an open heart" can now also be said of Tibet!

"And I sought for a man among them, that they should stand in the gap before me for the land that I should not destroy it—but I found none." Even as in the days of Ezekiel, so it is now! Many "gaps" are waiting to be filled in the world's great Mission fields.

And for Tibet? Who will lay courage, fortitude and talents at His feet? Who will offer for the King's service on the borders or in the interior of this vast land?

"For everyone without exception who calls on the name of the Lord shall be saved. But how are they to call on One in Whom they have not believed? And how are they to believe in One Whose voice they have never heard? *And how are they to hear without a preacher?*"[1]

[1] Weymouth's translation.

FACTS ABOUT THE C.I.M.

★ ★ ★

In the words of its founder, Hudson Taylor, who died in 1905, "The China Inland Mission was formed under a deep sense of China's pressing need, and with an earnest desire, constrained by the love of Christ and the hope of His coming, to obey His command to preach the Gospel to every creature."

Founded in 1865, the Mission has continued to grow, with God's blessing, until its missionaries number over 1,300, working in 339 centres in 19 provinces of China. There are well over 3,800 Chinese workers, including 2,300 men and women who voluntarily give the whole or part of their time to the work. The aim of the Mission is to found self-governing, self-supporting, and self-propagating churches throughout the whole of inland China. Chinese communicants number about 80,000.

The C.I.M. is a fellowship embracing members of all the principal denominations who "agree in the truth of God's Holy Word," and are therefore able to "live in unity and godly love." It is international in character, with its headquarters at Shanghai, and home centres in Great Britain, North America, and Australasia. In addition there are thirteen Associate Missions whose home centres are in Sweden, Norway, Germany, Finland, Denmark, and the United States, forming nearly one-third of the total membership of the Mission.

In regard to financial supplies the Mission is supported entirely by the freewill offerings of the Lord's people. No debt is incurred, no appeal for funds authorized, and its missionaries, whether on the field or on the home staffs, are dependent on God Himself—and not on the Mission—for the supply of their needs. But it may be stated to the glory of God that though there have been times of straitness He has never failed to meet the personal needs of the workers or the general needs of the work, and the amounts received in answer to prayer since the Mission was founded total nearly £5,000,000.

HOME DEPARTMENTS

★ ★ ★

The Prayer Union links together those who desire to pray systematically for the work. **The Prayer Companionship** provides individual missionaries with Companions who are pledged to pray regularly for the particular worker to whom they are attached.

The Deputation Department arranges for missionary services, meetings, and lantern lectures throughout the country.

Young people who feel the call to China are invited to correspond with the **Candidates' Secretary**. **The Home Preparation Union** provides a preparatory training for prospective candidates.

The Comradeship for China is the young people's branch of the Mission. Its Magazine, **Young China**, is published in alternate months, price 2d. per copy.

A list of **C. I. M. Publications** will be supplied on application. The official organ of the Mission is **China's Millions,** published monthly, price 2d. per copy, or 2s. 6d. per annum, post free. ($1 in North America).

The Medical Auxiliary assists medical workers on the field, and seeks to develop prayer circles, working parties, etc. at home.

Further information about any of these departments may be obtained on application to:

THE CHINA INLAND MISSION,
Newington Green, London, N.16.
16, Belmont Street, Glasgow, W.2.
237, W. School Lane, Germantown, Philadelphia.
150, St. George Street, Toronto 5, Ont.
64, Elizabeth Street, Melbourne.

SOME C.I.M. PUBLICATIONS

THE CALL OF CHINA'S GREAT NORTH-WEST
By MRS. HOWARD TAYLOR. *With map and illustrations.*
A graphic picture of Kansu and beyond. *Paper cover,* 1s. 6d. *net.*

THROUGH JADE GATE AND CENTRAL ASIA
By MISS A. M. CABLE and MISS F. FRENCH.
Cheap new edition, 3s. 6d. *net.*
A wonderful account of pioneer work and travel in Kansu and Turkestan.

DISPATCHES FROM NORTH-WEST KANSU
By MISS A. M. CABLE and MISS F. FRENCH. *Paper cover,* 9d. *net.*
A lively and telling little book on pioneer work in unevangelized regions.

THE RED LAMA
By MISS A. M. CABLE and MISS F. FRENCH.
An attractive new edition, 6d. *net.*
A thrilling story of a lama's first contact with the Gospel.

GEORGE KING, MEDICAL EVANGELIST
By THE REV. F. HOUGHTON, B.A. *Illustrated,* 2s. *net.*
The story of a doctor who sacrificed brilliant prospects to share not the Gospel of God only, but his own life also, with the people of China.

THE TWO HUNDRED
By THE REV. F. HOUGHTON, B.A. *Illustrated, paper cover,* 1s. *net.*
'A real up-to-date adventure story' which tells why The Two Hundred were needed, how they responded, who they are, and where they are now.

OUR SEAL
By MARSHALL BROOMHALL, M.A.
Crown 8vo., with illustrations and diagrams. Cloth, 2s. 6d. *net.*
A study of the financial experiences of the China Inland Mission from its inception, showing how, despite the test of time, of emergencies, of war, of exchange and of other extraordinary demands, the good Hand of God has been stretched out to supply every need.

HONEY TWO OF LISU-LAND
By MRS. A. B. COOKE.
With striking cover in colour and charming illustrations by Mr. Norman Baker.
Foolscap 8vo. 1s. *net.*
An attractive story of work amongst the Lisu tribe on the Yunnan-Burma border.

CHINESE IDYLLS
By THE REV. ROBERT GILLIES. *Art Cover,* 6d. *net.*
Fascinating stories of Chinese Christians.

Just Published.

THE BIBLE IN CHINA
By MARSHALL BROOMHALL, M.A.
Crown, 8vo. Illustrated. Cloth, 2s. 6d. *net.*
The fascinating story of the translation of God's Word into Chinese, and of the transformation of life which follows the acceptance of its claims.